Pasta Pronto!

ABOUT THE AUTHORS

PASTA PRONTO! is a family affair. The basic idea was developed by William E. Massee, who prefers the speedy kind of cooking exemplified in the recipes of the "Pasta Pronto" chapter. He is the author of six books on wine and food.

Dorothy Ivens (Massee) is responsible for the recipes in PASTA PRONTO! which require longer cooking but can be made ahead of time. Her most recent book is GLORIOUS STEW. A painter and illustrator, she has illustrated her own books, her husband's books, and PASTA PRONTO!

Original research and much of the recipe testing has been done by the Massees' daughter, Catherine Tremper, who started out testing recipes in the kitchen of *The New York Times*.

Pasta Pronto!

William E. Massee

with Dorothy Ivens and Catherine Tremper

CHL CREATIVE HOME LIBRARY

In Association with Better Homes and Gardens

Meredith Corporation

CHL CREATIVE HOME LIBRARY

© 1971 by Meredith Corporation, Des Moines, Iowa
SBN 696-36200-7   Library of Congress Number 72-145621
Printed in the United States of America

Cover design by Paul Bacon; photography by Paul Weller

Contents

PASTA PRONTO!

Pasta con Tre Formaggi
Pasta with Three Cheeses   55

Mozzarella, Gruyère, and Parmesan are the three cheeses which, with butter, make the sauce for this spaghetti. Still others are given as variations, including a fluffy ricotta, along with other things, such as sweet or sour cream.

Green Velvet Sauce   58

A smooth parsley sauce with garlic and olive oil, sharpened with vinegar.

Linguine con Salsa di Vongole, Bianca
Spaghetti with White Clam Sauce   60

Thin noodles with white clam sauce. Variations call for herbs, red pepper flakes, or lemon juice.

Vermicelli con Vongole, Salsa Rossa
Spaghetti with Red Clam Sauce   62

Clam sauce with tomatoes for thin spaghetti, and a variation calling for mussels.

Vermicelli con Acciughe
Spaghetti with Anchovies   64

Thin spaghetti with anchovy sauce, with lots of garlic and black olives. Variations include oregano, capers and mint, peppers or mushrooms, even tuna fish.

Spaghetti alla Salsa di Tonno
Spaghetti with Tuna Sauce   67

Tuna sauce, hearty or elegant, the light version here calling for mushrooms and a little tomato sauce with oil and butter, and sturdier variations calling for peas and onions or green peppers or chives.

Spaghetti à la Môde de Grand Mère
Spaghetti, Grandmother's Style   70

A novel sauce from French Switzerland, with little cubes of bacon or salt pork, ham and bread, cooked in butter until crisp and golden. Full of taste and texture.

Spaghettini all' Amatriciana
Spaghettini, Amatrice Style   72

Fine spaghetti with a sauce of olive oil, onion, salt pork or bacon, and tomatoes. Variations use white wine.

Trenette alla Carbonara
Noodles, Woodcutter's Way   75

A Roman dish of fine noodles made with bacon and ham, tossed with beaten eggs. Varied by using sausages instead of bacon and ham and adding mushrooms.

Spaghetti con Polpette
Spaghetti with Meatballs   105

Meatballs of ground beef cooked in tomato sauce. Variations for the meatballs include possible additions of capers, cheese, nuts, raisins, or olives, with substitution of fresh sage for parsley, and other meats for beef. Takes 1 hour to cook, but can be done ahead.

Ragú Bolognese
Bolognese Meat Sauce   108

Rich and luxurious sauce of ground beef with bacon, vegetables, wine, broth, tomatoes, and chicken livers, finished with cream. Cooks in 1½ hours. Can be done ahead, with cream added at last minute.

Friday Sauce   110

Simple, long-cooking marinara sauce of olive oil, garlic, tomatoes, oregano, salt, and pepper. Cooks in 1 hour.

PASTA AL FORNO—Assemblages of pasta, sauces, and other things, cooked separately and finished in the oven.

Lasagne   114
Broad bands of pasta baked with layers of Meat-and-Tomato Sauce and three cheeses—ricotta, mozzarella, and Parmesan.

Noodle Casserole   118

Moist noodle casserole, two layers with a filling of cottage cheese, cream cheese, sour cream, scallions, and green pepper, topped with Meat-and-Tomato Sauce.

Shell Noodles with Chili con Carne   121

Chili con Carne with the beef in chunks, used here in a casserole, with shell noodles rather than the customary kidney beans.

Shell Noodles with Curried Shrimp   124

Shrimp in a piquant curry sauce, combined in a casserole with shell noodles.

Macaroni and Cheese   127

Macaroni in a creamy cheese sauce, with green peppers and pimientos. Can have ham, seafood, and fish added—or, best of all, raw oysters.

Cannelloni and Manicotti
Stuffed Noodle Rolls   130

Stuffed pasta rolls, made with homemade noodle dough or packaged manicotti tubes, topped with Cream Sauce and Meat-and-Tomato Sauce. Two fillings given, one of cheese and spinach, another of ground beef.

PASTA CON BRIO—A collection of recipes for main dishes that call for pasta as a side dish.

CHINESE NOODLES AND OTHER FOREIGN AFFAIRS—Some notes on pasta around the world with recipes for a few favorites from China, Japan, Austria, Hungary, Germany, France, and the United States.

ANTIPASTI, INSALATI, AND DESSERTS—Various appetizers to serve before the pasta, and salads to serve with the meal or as a lunch or supper. Followed by light Italian classics to round out the meal.

Chef's Salad   180
Another main-course salad to go with pasta is the Chef's Salad with its ingredients of lettuce, cheese, ham, eggs, radishes, scallions, and a long list of variables.

Fruit   182
The best of all desserts whether the meal be pasta or pot roast. Includes suggestions for using liqueurs with fresh fruits.

Biscuit Tortoni   183
A frozen dessert laced with sherry and topped with almonds.

Zabaglione
Custard with Marsala   184
This spectacular dessert, flavored with Marsala, is a simple, light, and lovely custard that can be made at the table.

Poached Pears with Marsala   186
A cool, but spicy ending to any pasta meal.

INDEX   189

Introduction

Visitors arriving from abroad come bearing gifts. Some of the best of these are recipes. One summer, Holly flew in from Paris and sailed out to find some basil. My sister in Rome does this all the time, said Holly, chopping away.

Chop up ripe tomatoes and mash garlic cloves with teaspoonfuls of salt. Put everything in a big bowl, add a cup of chopped fresh basil, and stir with olive oil. Pour this over spaghetti and toss.

That's all. It's so light you can't believe it—and fresh tasting. A grinding of fresh pepper, if you like, and some grated Parmesan, but maybe it's better without the cheese. It should be salty, but we vary the salt, depending on how we feel. Makes you thirsty for wine, a white or rosé or even a coarse red. Some cheese and fruit, after, if you're starving. It's beautiful, all red and green.

But what's great about the recipe is—no cooking. You just dump everything in a bowl. You can do it all while the water boils.

We had pasta pronto all summer long.

PASTA PRONTO!

Some time in August we realized that several of the greatest pasta sauces needed no cooking, like Il Pesto of Genoa (page 52), which the kids took to calling Presto Pesto. Some sauces needed only warming, like Aglio e Olio (page 48). Others could be done in a chafing dish, like Fettuccine al Burro (page 44). Sauces we liked most could be done while the water's boiling and the pasta's cooking. And there were scores of variations for every sauce.

Take Sauce Ramatuelle (page 50), which is what Holly calls her sister's recipe, after the town on the French Riviera where they run a sort of open house for vagabond offspring of American friends. You can rub the bowl with a red chili pepper for a hint of hotness, or chop some up to rouse the languid guest, or just sprinkle in red pepper flakes to add authority. Slivers of green pepper add crunch. Some of the vagabonds liked a touch of chopped olives, and one liked scallions. Roman friends add anchovies to replace some of the salt. A French friend adds a dollop of yogurt on top. Set in our ways, we like it as we met it, fresh with the taste of tomatoes, redolent with basil, and salty for the wine.

We were beginning to learn a secret of the Italian genius with food. Even the simplest recipe can be varied, delightfully, so that it never tastes quite the same any time you prepare it. Cooking is not the main thing; what is central to Italian cuisine is the great flexibility of any pasta dish. Adding or changing an ingredient may enhance the basic taste or contrast with it, sometimes frankly or sometimes subtly, but always simply. Roving through the cookbooks we found dozens of recipes for the same thing, with different names, a little more oil or a little less, the garlic left in or taken out, or cream instead of milk, or a mild cheese for a sharp one, or a seasonal change from basil to oregano to parsley. This may be nowhere so manifest as in quick pasta dishes.

We used to have an offhand idea that pasta was mostly spaghetti and meatballs. Over the years we learned to love a sauce that was just a melted stick of butter with a teaspoonful of dried basil steeped in it, or a mess of clams steamed with white wine and poured over spaghetti with butter, garlic, and parsley. Nothing much more. There were so many other things to eat.

Sauce Ramatuelle opened us up and changed our ways.

Italian cooking is the mother cuisine of Europe; it borrows from the Greeks and Persians and the Orient, from the Moors and the Arabs, and was almost

14

revolutionized when tomatoes and red peppers and corn came in from the New World. Marie de Medici brought a developed cuisine to barbarian France. When only one aspect of it is considered, the genius shows, in all its vibrancy and gusto, not to be reduced to spaghetti and meatballs.

Not only can pasta pronto be done while the water is boiling and the pasta is cooking; it can offer an easy flexibility to a menu. Any one recipe can be a meal in itself, the flourish of tastes being quite satisfying when preceded by the bravura of antipasto or something cold, and followed by the scherzo of salad and cheese. It's easy to wax musical about Italian food. The simplest of desserts, like fresh fruit, round out the meal, but fancy desserts are a nice *glissando* before espresso and brandy.

Still better, pasta pronto can be a first course, to come before something simply barbecued or pan broiled or roasted. It can be the one hot dish served with a buffet. It can be prepared in a hurry, at the last minute, while having a round of drinks.

We are all so used to serving spaghetti as a main course we are apt to forget the Italian way of serving pasta as an introductory course. The reason may be that we think of spaghetti with a long-cooked meat-and-tomato sauce certainly hearty and satisfying, but monotonous—and heavy.

We tend to ignore the obvious—that a little starch cuts appetite fast, taking the edge off hunger so that we can enjoy other courses more, yet eat less of them. The mere pause between courses, as well as the variation from one dish to another, helps satisfy hunger, so that main courses are attractive with things other than potatoes and rice. Making the starch a separate course, even making pasta the side dish for a main course, serves to vary the meal. The novel, but still familiar, taste of a flavorsome pasta dish appeals to the hungry, even when small portions are served.

Pasta dishes come from times and places where meat was a luxury. Italian genius made a virtue of this, the bland nature of pasta serving as a foil for sharp sauces and delicacies, making such extravagant additions notable and provident. Playing up the additions becomes a virtue. The fact that pasta dishes can be prepared quickly is merely an added appeal.

Historically, the quick cooking of pasta had nothing to do with saving time for the cook, but with the shortage of firewood. Every nationality, including

15

Italian and Chinese, that has run out of fuel has developed a quick-cooking cuisine based on starch, which provides calories to warm the inner man. The Italians never threw out their hot water after cooking the pasta; instead, they would fork out the pasta and allow the water to cool; its evaporating steam provided a source of warmth for the surrounding space.

Spaghetti is no diet dish, having about as many calories as potatoes, rice, bread, or an apple. But the pronounced flavors of a sauce makes it more satisfying to those on a calorie regimen. A pound of spaghetti will serve four people plentifully as a main course, and often six or even eight when the sauce is full of taste. Half a pound will serve four as a first course or a side dish, and sometimes six if the sauce is full of bits and pieces.

Having grown so used to the way spaghetti is served in American restaurants, it was a revelation to discover that there can be a lightness to pasta dishes. Pasta often arrives in a gloppy mass, overcooked and scarcely steaming, with a skimpy dribble of sauce in the center. The friendly neighborhood spaghetti joint serves the sauce in the middle of a soggy swirl to show you are getting some. By the time you've twirled the sauce into the pasta and added cheese, the plateful is cooler than lukewarm.

The trick is in the tossing of the pasta.

To watch an Italian tossing spaghetti at home is tantalizing. He wants it hot, so the bowl is warmed in the oven while the pasta finishes cooking; or some hot water may be poured into the bowl and then poured out just before the spaghetti comes off the stove. As often as not, a tablespoon of oil or lump of butter is then put in the warm bowl. The spaghetti, cooked just to bitiness so that no white center remains in a strand, is drained and poured into the bowl. Some of the sauce, or all of it, goes in, and tossing begins.

With a big fork in one hand and a big spoon in the other, the cook raises the spaghetti beneath the sauce a couple of inches and carefully rolls it over the sauce. Lifting and turning, lifting and turning, he aims to coat every strand. Occasionally, he dips to the bottom of the bowl to incorporate any sauce that has dribbled through. Sometimes, he will push down deep on both sides of the bowl, lifting perhaps half the mass and folding it over, the way one tosses a salad.

It is a deliberate performance, repeated again and again. The smell is

16

mouth-watering. Surely, that's enough. He's trying to get air into it. It must be cooling off. He's turning it half a dozen times more than seems necessary. The sauce has almost disappeared. Now he's turning it out on plates. Has everybody got some? There . . . delicious—and still hot.

Getting air into the spaghetti requires a slow-motion deftness like that of a good carver. The tosser looks as if he is trying to recapture the steam that comes off the pile. Lifting the strands too high or hastily will cool them.

Alfredo of Rome gave such a performance when tossing pasta that Mary Pickford and Douglas Fairbanks gave him a golden fork and spoon to add grandeur to the flourish. A spotlight played on him as he tossed. He retired from his restaurant in the forties but couldn't stand being without an audience so he opened another, Alfredo all'Augusto, to get back to his tossing. He had to get a new golden fork and spoon because the original Alfredo alla Scrofa was using the other pair.

Alfredo's famous dish is made by slicing a pound of butter into a pound of those thin hot noodles called fettuccine, tossing gently as the butter melts and incorporating a pound of freshly grated Parmesan. The dish is richly creamy beyond imagining. But light. And hot.

We thought it was a little too rich. So we added, to the noodles, only a half a pound of butter and of cheese and poured in a quarter cup of milk. We got a certain creaminess, but it wasn't quite as good. We tried sour cream; not as rich and not the same. We learned to vary the creaminess to suit the moment, and to serve small portions.

Exploring once begun, it became a game to find other recipes that could be prepared while the pasta boils. Some had an Oriental touch, which led to stir-frying and keeping in stock such things as bean sprouts and palm hearts, ginger and soy sauce. But this was far afield. There were Italian sauces that could be cooked ahead, in large batches, and frozen, so that even these could be used to make pasta pronto. With such sauces on hand, delights like lasagne and cannelloni could be made ahead of time, and finished in the oven at the last minute. There were all the dishes that could be served with or after pasta—stews and pot roasts that could be done ahead of time, sautées that could be done at the last minute. There was what to serve before pasta—antipasto—and the salads that could follow. And the wines to accompany.

All this is a long way from spaghetti and meatballs. Any Italian will tell you so. Columbus showed Europe a new world. Italians were explorers centuries before that. It's a gift.

WINES FOR PASTA

Pasta calls for wine, cool whites sharp and fresh in the leafy shade of the patio, tangy reds gurgling into the glasses on the checkered tablecloth, long swallows between mouthfuls, then sips with the cheese. Fruit then, and grappa with the coffee. And maybe before the meal, vermouth and soda, with lots of tinkling ice, and a twist of lemon for tang. Pasta calls for wine, in all its forms.

A gentleman from Turino invented vermouth in the eighteenth century, although the flowers of wormwood had been used to flavor wine since Grecian days. Wormwood was used to hide off-tastes, then, along with other flowers and herbs and honey. Runners brought snow down from the mountains to cool the wines, and there was an art to mixing the herbs and sweeteners. Having hit the right proportions, measure for measure, the gentleman left for Germany and there his concoction was named. The Italians kept the formula, and eventually two vermouths were made from red wines—one that was bitter and used sparingly, one that was sweet and drunk whenever anybody wanted to sit down and talk. If the café was not invented to serve the dark brew of the Turks, then it was surely created to provide a glass of vino or vermouth. Long before coffee, the *trattoria* drew the populace to its tables—the very word means pull or attraction—and the taverna existed in the time of the Etruscans. Whatever else, there was always wine in Italy.

The drink known as Americano, named perhaps to attract the tourist, calls for equal parts of sweet and bitter vermouth, with soda and a lemon twist, in a tall glass with ice. There's the Negroni, devised by the Roman hotel to please the traveler, gin replacing the sweet vermouth. Visiting English developed Gin and It, half sweet vermouth and gin, with ice. Italians are mostly satisfied with vermouth as it comes, maybe with ice.

But the above drinks are merely preparation for the feast. It is the wonders of the wine cellar that we are concerned with here, and from Italy comes a variety unequaled anywhere. Every town, it seems, has its own wines, dry reds and whites, sweet whites, some with a few bubbles called *frizzante,* others with many, called *spumante.* There are wines called *amabile,* amiable wines that are light and sweet and pleasing to drink cold on a hot day. Wines gush everywhere, from all manner of grapes, for every mood.

The best come from the north, from the slopes that lead up to the Alps—the big reds of the Piedmont, the lighter reds and rosés of Lombardy, the whites from north of Venice. From the countryside around Verona come the best white, Soave, and fresh young reds of Valpolicella and Bardolino. From Tuscany, south of Florence, comes Chianti, and still others on the way to Rome, and in the Roman hills, and more from Naples and the islands. You need a list.

Pasta calls for wine you swallow, not just sip, full of taste but easy to drink. Practically all Italian wines are at their best when young and fruity. A few attain a certain elegance with age—the best of Piedmont's Barolos and Barbarescos, the Chianti Classicos that are put in regular wine bottles. Some of these may take six years to round out, and are called roast wines—*vini per arrosto*—because they are meant to be served with roasts, but even such special bottlings are delicious with rich or creamy pastas, and regular bottlings are just right for meat sauces not dominated by tomatoes.

Chianti Chianti Soave Verdicchio Valpolicella

PASTA PRONTO!

The sharpness of tomatoes spoils the taste of wines, it is said, and this is certainly so when a sauce is harsh and heavy and the wine is light and delicate. But a good tomato sauce is rarely harsh, its pungency muted by the blandness of the pasta. Few Italian wines are so delicate that they will not glorify a dish of pasta. Their fruitiness and depth of taste bring out the best of what's in the dish.

Like those of other countries, Italian wines are known by the districts from which they come or the grapes from which they are made. The list below starts with the best, the wines from the northern province called the Piedmont, then proceeds south, with grape names indicated when they appear on the labels. Perhaps a score of Italian reds come into the United States, maybe half a dozen whites. We could wish for fifty. American wines that are similar are listed with each group, then these are summarized in a separate list.

PIEDMONT REDS

Vineyards on the slopes above the upper reaches of the Po River produce two of the best Italian reds. Barolo is pungent and robust and dark, almost purple; many of the best bottles bear the mark, a golden lion on a blue field, of the local control group, the *consorzio*. Barbaresco is somewhat lighter and less pungent, some of the best bearing a seal of an old tower. Both are made from the Nebbiolo grape, as are several others. The Freisa grape is planted in the townships of Asti and Chieri to make a light and perfumed red wine. The Grignolino grape makes a dry, light-colored red. The Barbera produces a rough and robust red that is delicious when young. This grape does even better in California, where it produces perhaps the best Italianesque wine made on the West Coast, while Grignolino in California makes a light red and an excellent fruity rosé.

Barolo	Freisa
Barbaresco	Grignolino
Gattinara	Barbera
Carema	Dolcetto

20

LOMBARDY REDS

The country north of Milan produces distinguished wines from Nebbiolo grapes planted in the valley of Valtellina east of Lake Como. Lighter than Piedmont wines and hard when young, they come from hillsides known as Sassella, Grumello, and Inferno and are usually so identified on labels. In the south, near Pavia, the Burgundian grape, Pinot Noir, is planted along with others, and the best-known wine is marketed under the brand name, Frecciarossa. California wines from the Pinot Noir grape present a good alternative.

Sassella
Grumello
Inferno

VERONA REDS

The home of Romeo and Juliet is in the province of Veneto and boasts two districts that make delicious light and fruity reds. The best is Bardolino, above the shores of Lake Garda. Others are the more variable Valpolicella, over the hills to the east, and Valpantena. Soft California reds from the Gamay Beaujolais or Petite Syrah might be served instead.

Bardolino   Valpantena
Valpolicella   Chiaretto Rosato

TUSCANY REDS

Chianti is perhaps the most famous wine in the world, produced in vineyards south of Florence. The best is supposedly denominated as Chianti Classico, from a group of towns whose wines are marketed with a seal showing a cock in a black ring. Others, equally good Chiantis come from outside the district, and some of these use a seal showing a white cherub. The range of Chianti wines is wide and brands are important. The wines have a sprightly quality, a liveliness that comes from putting some overripe grapes in with the fermenting wine; the practice is called

21

governo. Young Chiantis, in their straw baskets known as *fiascos,* are fresh and delightful, older ones that are usually marketed in regular bottles have a certain elegance.

This characteristic of being good to drink when young or old is shared by the California wine, Zinfandel. This California red is quite different from Chianti, but equally good and frequently better, particularly when it comes from Napa or Sonoma, Santa Clara or Monterey. Chianti varies considerably so that brand names are important: distinguished names are the Brolio or Meleto of Ricasoli, Machiavelli, and Antinori.

OTHER REDS

Red wines come from everywhere in Italy, and the best is always the local wine on the table, some of which can be remarkable. A grower may sell all his production to a restaurant or two, so that it never becomes available elsewhere, and this is one of the joys of traveling in Italy. Some have more than local interest. A famous red comes from the Italian Tyrol north of Venice, Santa Maddalena; it is soft and fruity when made well. Lambrusco comes from just west of Bologna, where it is popular because of its fruitiness and full aroma, but it has a sweetish and slightly sparkling quality that is not always appealing. From near Naples comes soft and fruity Gragnano, and further south, from the slopes of Monte Vulture, comes the Aglianico del Vulture, rare but full, with a rich bouquet. Any of these is hard to find, outside Italy.

WHITE WINES

The white wines of Italy are usually soft, even when dry, and are best when less than three years old. In each district, grapes are allowed to dry after being picked, and made into sweet wines called *passito;* many are sparkling. The drier whites are delicious with pastas that are creamy, contain ham or fowl, fish or seafood, particularly the latter. The best white from the Piedmont is the

Cortese from Gavi. White Lugana comes from near Lake Garda. But these are hard to find in this country.

Soave comes from Verona. It is the best white wine of Italy, when made well, outranking Orvieto, which is the white companion of Chianti from vineyards farther south. The hills of Rome provide Frascati, and over toward the Adriatic are the Castelli di Jesi and light, fresh wines from the Verdicchio grape. Verdicchio has an earthy taste when not of the best. The whites from Capri and Ischia are celebrated, so much so that little of it leaves the islands. There is also the Etna of Sicily, as well as its Corvo. On Sardinia, the Vernaccia grape produces a powerful white wine that is aromatic; there is Cinque Terre from the Italian Riviera that is usually sweet. The most familiar whites come from the Italian Tyrol, made from German grapes like Riesling and Traminer. These are excellent but hard to find, as are wines from the Terlano grape. In most instances, the white wines of California and New York State are equally interesting.

Soave	Frascati
Orvieto	Verdicchio
Chianti Bianco	Vernaccia

AMERICAN WINES

A wave of immigration from Italy toward the end of the nineteenth century brought many winemakers to California, so that much of the common red wine made there today is made in a somewhat Italianate style. Many of them bear Italian-sounding names, among them Barberone, Vino di Tavola, Vino Tipo, and Chianti. Wines with such borrowed names are worth trying because they are cheap, if bland. Few of them are in the same class as California wines called Mountain Red or Mountain White, generic names for blends of wines that are California's own.

Better wines from California are marketed under grape names. Examples are Zinfandel, Grignolino, and Barbera, all of them excellent red wines for most pastas that call for reds. These are superior to the stream of ordinary Italian wines that come into the United States, and even match some of the best bottlings from Piedmont, Lombardy, Verona, and Tuscany.

The best of the California red varietals are made from French grapes, light and elegant wines that surpass many of those from Italy. These are sold by various producers, marketed as Cabernet Sauvignon, Pinot Noir, Gamay Beaujolais, and Petite Syrah. The first two are almost too elegant for all but the most subtle sauces like Ragú Bolognese (page 108).

The white wines of California are superior to all but the very best Italian whites. The most distinguished is Chardonnay, which is often called Pinot Chardonnay on labels, because of an old idea that it was of the Pinot grape family; it is not, but the Pinot Blanc is. And a grape called the White Pinot in California is really the French Chenin Blanc; and the wine is marketed under both names. All this is confusing, but there is no way around the difficulty, except tasting the wines—which are excellent—and picking the ones you like. Other California white wines from French grapes are Sauvignon Blanc and Sémillon, also excellent.

The best California white from German grapes is called Johannisberg Riesling. Others are called Grey Riesling and Emerald Riesling, which can be good. Still another is called, simply, Riesling, a wine that is actually made from a Rhineland grape, the Sylvaner, and this can also be a pleasant wine. All of them are excellent with light pastas, particularly those that include fish or shellfish.

New York State produces an excellent red wine from a hybrid grape called Baco Noir. However, the best wines of the state are white. One from native grapes is called Delaware. European grapes in New York are used mostly for blends, but a Rhineland grape, Gewürztraminer, produces some remarkable wines. So does the Chardonnay, but its wines are hard to find.

For quick reference, we present a list of outstanding American wines.

24

California Reds	*California Whites*
Cabernet Sauvignon	Chardonnay or Pinot Chardonnay
Pinot Noir	Pinot Blanc
Zinfandel	Johannisberg Riesling
Gamay Beaujolais	Chenin Blanc or White Pinot
Barbera	Sauvignon Blanc
Petite Syrah	Sémillon
New York Red	*New York Whites*
Baco Noir	Delaware
	Gewürztraminer

ITALIAN FORTIFIED WINES, BRANDIES, AND LIQUEURS
Italy produces enormous quantities of brandy, the distillate of wine, and uses it to stabilize and fortify certain wines. The best known fortified wine is Marsala, which is something like a lightly sweetened Spanish sherry. Marsala is used mostly in cooking.

The brandies alone are mostly drunk, quite casually, with coffee or in it. Few approach the excellence of the Cognacs and Armagnacs of France, but the Italians rarely make the fuss about drinkables that the French do, being thankful for what they have. However, various restaurants throughout Italy have special hoards of old brandies that are worth asking for.

A special distillate is grappa, distilled from the crushed pulp left in the press after the juice has been expressed from the grapes. Grappa is strong and usually colorless, although it picks up a brandy tinge when left to age in casks. It has a taste best described as leathery. A version called *ruta* is occasionally found, which is made by steeping a sprig of rue in a bottle of newly distilled grappa. Ruta has a surprising and refreshing taste but, unlike grappa, is rarely exported.

The Italians also produce a wide range of liqueurs and cordials. Perhaps the most popular are those flavored with anise, the taste of licorice being an excellent foil to espresso coffee. A

25

sweet liqueur that is exported is one made from that variety of cherry called Maraschino; the best versions are colorless. Many sweet herb-flavored liqueurs are made, the most familiar being Strega and Galliano. Also popular is Fior d'Alpi, which is usually marketed with a branch of rock candy in the bottle.

The pleasure in all this, of course, is exploring whatever is available, particularly the wines. The very nature of pasta encourages discovery. May you vary the wine as often as the sauce.

COOKING AND MAKING THE SAUCE

Italians put all sorts of things in sauces, some of them strange to foreigners not used to eating pasta every day. Italy's national colors could be symbols of this kind of cooking—green for herb sauces of the north, red for tomato sauces of the south, the white band in the middle for pasta. What else goes in is like the flaunting breeze that makes the banner wave.

THE SAUCE AND THE BATTUTO

Most sauces begin with mashing and chopping, but instead of chopping each item separately, an Italian chops them together, starting with fresh herbs so flavors mingle subtly. This blending is called *battuto;* when cooked it becomes the *soffrito.* (Americans usually have dried herbs that go in later, so the practice is rarely followed here.) *Battuto* seems to be a mutation of the Chinese method of cutting materials into bits before cooking, so that they can be eaten with chopsticks after quick cooking. A chopper with a curved blade, called the *mezzaluna,* is used. The half-moon shape has an Oriental look. The flat of the blade is used for mashing. When all is chopped to the desired size, the *battuto* is scraped into hot fat.

THE FAT

Northern Italy is the land of butter, the south is olive oil country. Butter and oil mingle in Tuscany and spread out from there.

Oil is supposed to impart silkiness to a sauce, not heaviness. Butter adds richness, and because it smokes at lower temperatures than oil, some oil is usually added to keep the butter from burning. Pasta, like rice or potatoes or bread, needs some fat to taste good and to help spread the sauce on and through the strands, but never so much as to mask the flavors of the sauce. Bacon, ham, or salt pork are often used with the oil or butter to blend flavors; these ingredients also add saltiness or crisp texture.

THE LIQUID

Pasta *asciutta* is the overall term for spaghetti or noodles with sauce (meaning "dry" only in contrast to pasta *in brodo,* which is pasta in broths or soups like minestrone).

Pasta that doesn't have enough sauce is horrible. A pound of spaghetti may call for two or more cups of sauce, perhaps half of it being liquid. Oil or butter provides enough moistness for many sauces; tomatoes provide enough wetness in others. When a sauce needs to be extended, you can thin it with milk or cream or stock—enough so that a sprinkle of cheese will melt readily. When in doubt about the amount, Italian cooks have been known to add wine, red or white, to a possibly skimpy sauce.

Italians like the pasta itself to be moist but not gloppy. The first control is not to drain the pasta too much; some of the boiling water may be set aside for adding, if necessary. The second is to put a little butter or oil, or both, in the warmed bowl into which the drained spaghetti is poured. After the sauce is added to the pasta, and tossed, a little more oil or butter may be added. It is better to err on the side of generosity.

GARLIC AND ONIONS

Garlic presents itself in many sauces, particularly those from southern Italy; and its pungency is imparted in many ways. Some cooks press the cloves lightly before putting them into the hot fat; this adds just a whiff of flavor. Others press the cloves

27

repeatedly after they go into the fat, so that much of their oils are given up. To add more pungency, still others mash the cloves with the flat of a knife, or chop then finely, or grind them with salt in a saucer, using a fork. There are cooks that sliver the garlic and let it brown before removing it. Some cooks always remove the garlic after cooking it; others leave it in. Garlic browns quickly and can impart a burned taste; you should cook it until soft or just golden, then add other ingredients promptly to cool the oil and keep the garlic from scorching.

Onions, sliced or chopped, are frequently added with the garlic. They are cooked only until transparent or limp or golden. They lend sweetness, smoothness, and savor to sauces.

Scallions, variously called green onions or spring onions, and members of the onion family, like shallots or leeks, are cooked scarcely at all in most sauces, to allow their freshness and aromatic qualities to come through. Chives, the most delicate of all, are sometimes used as a garnish. In most sauces, members of the onion family are meant to add to the orchestration of the whole, not to dominate.

TOMATOES

Tomatoes came to Europe from the New World and became the rage of Naples, the pasta center of Italy; later, hard times in Italy drove people back across the Atlantic with their recipes. The first tomatoes to reach Italy were yellow and were called *pomodòro*, but this "golden apple" was supplanted by red varieties, from which was developed the Italian plum tomato, named for its shape. No nation uses tomatoes in as many ways as Italy; some say too many.

Fresh tomatoes cooked for less than three minutes in a skillet whose bottom has been covered with oil or butter make the freshest tasting sauce of all for pasta. At five minutes fresh tomatoes become orange rather than red, and provide a satiny and rich-tasting sauce. Fresh tomatoes separate after five minutes, becoming watery, and don't begin to thicken again until after fifteen minutes cooking time, and are a perfect, smooth sauce when they have cooked about twenty minutes. Four cups of chopped tomatoes will reduce to about two cups after twenty minutes of cooking; they become further reduced and more concentrated in taste if the cooking continues.

Skin and seeds add a certain rough texture that is desirable in many quick and simple sauces. Because seeds lend a bitter taste after long cooking, they are often removed before cooking by squeezing the tomatoes through the fingers or by pressing them through a sieve. Some cooks automatically peel and seed tomatoes, dipping them first in hot water for a few seconds so that the skin comes off easily.

Tomatoes should be cooked in enamelware because they can pick up a metallic taste from ironware. The heat should be kept just below the point where the tomatoes plop and splash all over the place, a tendency that increases as the tomatoes reduce.

Canned Italian plum tomatoes go through much the same transformation during cooking as do fresh ones, but first must be drained. If they are not drained, they taste watery and take longer to cook. They are most easily seeded by forcing them through a sieve or food mill. Italian plum tomatoes are canned with a basil leaf and seasonings, unlike most American canned tomatoes. When drained, they can be used almost interchangeably with fresh tomatoes.

Canned tomato purée is smooth, without seeds or skins, and is usually canned without seasonings. It is good to use when only a little tomato taste or color is wanted.

Canned tomato sauce varies from brand to brand. Most of them are excellent when tomatoes are a minor element in a sauce or dish, but can't compare with fresh or canned tomatoes that have been reduced. The seasoning is mild, and generally has to be

29

corrected for pasta sauces, by adding pepper and herbs like oregano or basil; oil or butter may be needed for smoothness.

Canned tomato paste is very concentrated. It has a strong metallic taste unless cooked for at least an hour. It is a necessary ingredient in many long-cooking sauces. Tomato paste contains no noticeable seasonings.

HERBS AND SEASONINGS

Fresh herbs are the prime ingredient for pasta sauces. The most prized herb is basil, familiarly called *la erbe,* as if there were no other. Basil is a favorite herb of southern Italy, where even the province at the instep of the boot is called Basilicata; it is prized in Genoa, where it is the essence of the greatest of uncooked sauces, Il Pesto (page 52). Basil can be simply steeped in oil to make one sauce, which is varied by adding parsley, garlic, and butter—all or just one or two. Italians say that the basil leaves should be stroked, then torn apart to release most flavor, a comment usually made with the cock of an eyebrow. Northern Italians who are not Genoese may state that basil is too bitter when used by itself or in large amounts; they will urge the merits of leafy Italian parsley, oregano, or the less pungent marjoram or thyme.

Preference in this book is always for fresh herbs, used alone or with another, usually parsley. Dried herbs can be used when fresh ones aren't in the market. Dried herbs are always much stronger; a teaspoon of the dried is about equal to a tablespoon of the fresh. Dried herbs can be steeped with a tablespoonful or so of hot water, but are generally simply added to a sauce toward the end of the cooking time.

Salt is used generously in most sauces to counteract the blandness of the pasta. Some cooks heavily salt the water in which the pasta cooks, going light on salt in the sauce. A squeeze of lemon sometimes goes into a sauce at the end, to add piquancy. Grilled or sautéed meats are invariably served with a wedge of lemon, a

Italian Parsley

Basil

few drops squeezed over them to freshen the taste and cut any excess of butter or oil.

Freshly ground black pepper is commonly used. Red pepper flakes are often added for hotness. Fresh red peppers are frequently chopped into a sauce or merely rubbed around the bowl in which the pasta is to be tossed.

Capers, pimientos, olives, croutons, anchovies, nuts—all are added to pasta dishes, but one or two at a time. The aim is always to embellish the main taste, as harmony or contrast. Pasta calls for variety when it is a daily mealtime dish. Less frequent pasta eaters might think a sauce of freshly sautéed zucchini or eggplant, peas or asparagus, is odd and unspectacular. An Italian finds it a welcome change. A cook will vary a favorite sauce, just for the surprise, and the diners admire her imagination. Wit and whim are part of every good pasta.

CHEESE

Most pasta dishes call for a grating of cheese on top. Many incorporate cheese in the sauce. A good selection of Italian cheeses can be found in America, ranging from sharp and tangy, through mild and creamy, to fresh; they are often used in combination.

31

People tend to steer clear of the strong cheeses, dreading the bite, but strong cheeses are reduced to a subtle flavor by the bland pasta; these strong cheeses may be available only in specialty shops.

Tangy cheese for grating, which are sharp when aged, include:

Parmigiano—Called Parmesan when it is made in America, named after its town of origin, it is the most popular of all grating cheese. Versions of this mellow cheese are called *grana.*

Pecorino—Tangy, called the king of grating cheeses. The most famous version is Pecorino Romano.

Sardo—A Genoese favorite because of its salty sharpness. From Sardinia.

Ricotta Siciliana—An aged kind of cream cheese that is particularly spicy.

Strong cheeses for grating, used alone over pungent sauces, or in combination with milder cheeses, include:

Caciocavallo—Sharp Sicilian cheese that dates back to the Middle Ages. Spindle shaped.

Ragusano—Spicy and more subtle than the above, made from cow's milk. Shaped like a log.

Incanestrata—Also called Canestrata. Salty and biting, a peppery version is called pepato. Named for its basket shape.

Mild cheeses are used for creamy sauces or in concert with sharper cheeses, and include:

Fontina—Like the Gruyère or Emmenthaler of Switzerland. American Swiss is similar.

Fonduta—Like Germany's Münster.

Ricotta Romana—Lightly salty. Similar to our cottage cheese.

Fresh cheeses that are soft and creamy are used in some pasta sauces, but their widest use is as fillings for cannelloni, manicotti, and ravioli:

32

Mozzarella—Smooth and delicate, like a soft Gouda.

Mascarpone—An Italian cream cheese. Also called robiola.

Ricotta—Like a smooth cottage cheese, fluffy when whipped, and extremely mild when fresh.

Table cheeses are rarely used for pastas and sauces, but Italians produce some of the best, eating them with antipasto or with fresh fruit at the end of a meal. Some table cheeses are:

Bel Paese—Mellow and rich.

Taleggio—Mellow, rich, and creamy like butter. Similar to the French Brie.

Provolone—A mild cheese when young, customarily served as part of the antipasto.

Gorgonzola—An excellent blue cheese, perhaps Italy's best. There is a milder, white version.

MAKING YOUR OWN PASTA

Making pasta is as rewarding as making your own bread. Nothing compares. And it is easy. The trick is to let the dough rest for ten minutes before kneading. It's as simple as one, two, three.

Homemade Egg Noodles
1 teaspoon salt
2 cups flour
3 eggs
4 tablespoons water

Dump the flour into a bowl or on a board and make a hole in the center. Sprinkle the salt into the hole, then break the eggs into it. Stir the eggs into the flour with fork or fingers, and when the dough begins to lump, work it into a ball with your hands. A little water may be needed, depending on the dampness in the air. If the dough is sticky because you have added too much water, sprinkle over it a little more flour. It will be a very firm ball.

Flatten it a few times, pushing and folding it over. Press into a ball again and cover it with a cloth.

Wait ten minutes.

Sprinkle the board with flour and knead the dough a little longer than you want to—about ten minutes. Think of kneading as a pleasure: flatten the ball with the heels of the palms, fold the dough over on itself, turn it a quarter of the way around, flatten again, fold and turn, and so on. Do this until the dough is smooth and elastic—and no longer rubbery. Sprinkle or lightly sift a little flour over the dough if it is at all sticky. Cover the dough.

Wait five minutes.

Divide the dough into four balls, flatten them out, and roll out each in turn. The sheets should be thin, somewhat less than a sixteenth of an inch. (The edges are apt to be thinner than the middle of the sheet; this should be avoided.)

Smooth some flour over each sheet with your hand, then roll it up like a jelly roll. Slice off rounds across the roll, about a quarter-of-an-inch wide. Unroll each strand and lay it on a kitchen towel to dry for half an hour. This makes about a pound of uncooked noodles.

VARIATIONS ON HOMEMADE PASTA DOUGH
—Homemade pasta dough can be varied endlessly. It can be made only with flour and water. More eggs can be used, or fewer eggs and more water. The addition of oil makes a more tender dough. Here is an excellent variation of the above recipe that will give you two pounds of noodles:

    4 cups flour
    3 eggs
    2 tablespoons olive oil
    1 teaspoon salt
    some water, perhaps ¼ cup

The olive oil makes the dough easier to handle, too, so you do

34

not have to wait ten minutes after mixing the dough before you knead it. However, the dough should rest for ten minutes after kneading. Once the tender dough has been rolled out it will be easier to handle if each sheet is dusted with cornmeal, then smoothed with the hand. This helps to dry the sheet. After being cut, the strands can be spread to dry on a board dusted with cornmeal.

—A recipe that comes with our pasta machine calls for starting with 4 cups of flour, to which are added 4 tablespoons of milk, 3 eggs, 2 tablespoons of olive oil, and only a pinch of salt.

—A chef on the Italian steamship line uses a little less flour, leaves out the oil, and substitutes white wine for the milk.

—Green noodles have a special appeal, mostly because of their color, although they do seem to have a slightly different taste. They are made of using a purée of spinach instead of water:

> 4 cups flour—semolina, unbleached, or all-purpose
> 3 eggs
> 2 tablespoons olive oil
> 1 teaspoon salt
> 1 pound cooked spinach, fresh or frozen, drained and finely chopped into a purée, then squeezed very dry.

Make a dough by adding eggs, olive oil, and salt to the flour. Mix in the spinach, adding more flour if the dough is sticky. One cup of spinach is enough to color the dough, so leftover spinach can be used if you have it. Parsley or watercress can be used instead of the spinach, and need not be cooked beforehand, but must be very finely chopped and squeezed dry.

SOME TRICKS TO MAKING DOUGH

Italians generally knead the dough right away after mixing it, instead of letting it rest for ten minutes. They consider this produces a better dough, but kneading is much easier when you wait, and the result is excellent.

The Italians use the hard flour, semolina, for making pasta dough, considering this the best. When it is not available, all-purpose flour can be used, and makes good noodles; unbleached flour produces noodles with a better taste.

A pasta machine is a great help in the kneading. One costs about twenty-five dollars and is an excellent investment. A ball of dough is passed a few times between smooth rollers that can be set closer and closer together. The result is a smooth and even sheet that is cut in strips by passing the dough between sets of edged rollers. Most machines have rollers that cut the sheets into quarter-inch strips, like the noodles called tagliatelle or fettuccine, and a finer size about one-eighth of an inch wide, like the matchstick noodles of Genoa—trenette. Other sizes are available, but these are the most desirable. Only noodles can be made on a pasta machine; round spaghetti is made on commercial machines by forcing the dough through dies.

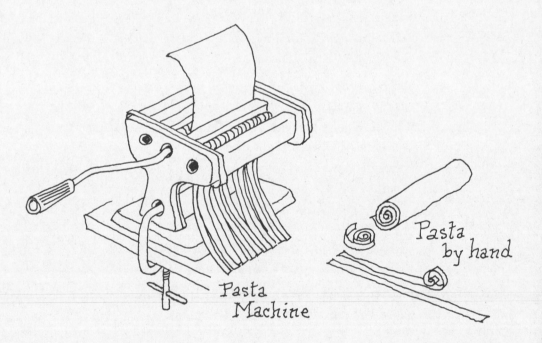

Pasta Machine

Pasta by hand

OTHER USES OF HOMEMADE PASTA DOUGH

Sheets of homemade pasta dough are most commonly made into noodles, wide or narrow, but they can also be made into wide strips for lasagne. Cut into various shapes, the dough can be used for a variety of filled pastas, cannelloni being the easiest to make.

Cannelloni (page 130) are small squares or oblongs of pasta dough three or four inches on a side. A filling is placed on the center of the sheet, which has been cooked, then it is rolled up, covered with sauces and a sprinkle of cheese, then put in the oven to get hot.

Ravioli (page 134) is a most familiar form of dough, a sort of cushion made by spacing spoonfuls of a filling on a large sheet of dough, covering this with another sheet, then cutting them apart.

Agnolotti are cooked circles of dough on which a spoonful of filling is placed; the dough is then folded over to make a half circle. The edges are pressed together, then they are covered with a sauce and heated in the oven. They can also be treated like ravioli, just boiled in water, then buttered and sauced.

Tortellini (page 135) are circles of dough that are filled and folded over, then the ends are pinched together; like an agnolotti, but smaller.

Pasta, finally, is just what you want it to be, like most things Italian, in or out of the kitchen. The homemade dough is so good that, once made, it is hard to go back to packaged noodles.

PACKAGED PASTA

Store-bought pasta is generally very good, particularly the kinds imported from Italy, where the flour is somewhat different from ours. There are more than a hundred shapes and sizes of pasta; this can be confusing, so we list the ones you are most likely to come across in stores or restaurants.

Something worth noting is that a sauce tastes different with different sizes of pasta, depending on the amount of sauce picked up. Generally, thin sauces taste best with thin forms of pasta, thick, with thick. Thin noodles seem to call for thin or creamy sauces, odd shapes call for thick sauces. Varying the size and shape of the pasta can be an attractive way to vary a meal.

All good pastas are the color of ivory when made from white flour, or an even deeper yellow when eggs are part of the dough. Those that look grayish, like putty or concrete, are generally poor quality. A pasta should feel smooth, not sandy or powdery, should be springy when fresh, should snap cleanly when dry; it should not crumble or splinter.

Spaghetti is the commonest form of pasta, round strands about an eighth of an inch in diameter.

Vermicelli, meaning little worms, are thin strands of spaghetti, sometimes sold in clusters.

Spaghettini are strands thinner than spaghetti, less than an eighth of an inch across.

Linguine are flattened strands of spaghetti, usually thin.

Noodles are ribbons of pasta. Wide ribbons have ruffled edges, called *riccie.*

Trenette are thin ribbons, thick as a matchstick.

Fettuccine are ribbons about a quarter of an inch wide.

Tagliatelle are like fettuccine, but may be three quarters of an inch across.

Lasagne may be two inches wide.

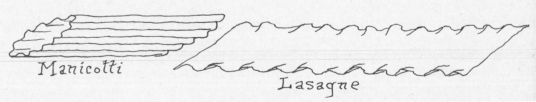

Manicotti

Lasagne

Maccheroni is the Italian term for all pasta, but the English word "macaroni" means pasta tubes. These may be short or long, thick or thin, curved or straight. *Rigati* added to the names of various kinds means that they are ribbed. Those listed below can be found in most supermarkets.

Bucatini are tubes about as thick as spaghetti.

Mezzani means medium in size and are about a quarter of an inch in diameter, the most familiar size of macaroni.

Ziti means bridegrooms, and are tubes about half an inch thick.

Mastaccioli are short tubes, called moustaches.

Tufoli are short tubes an inch thick, meant to be stuffed.

Manicotti are also meant to be stuffed, the tubes being an inch thick. They are usually ribbed, with ends cut at an angle.

Rigatoni are large ribbed tubes like manicotti, meant for stuffing.

Fancy shapes are numbered in the dozens; once rarely seen outside Italian neighborhoods, but now appearing in supermarkets, they are best with hearty sauces.

Conchiglie or *maruzze* are shells, small or large. Big sizes are meant to be stuffed.

Farfalle are butterflies or bows that come in various sizes.

Fusilli are twisted strands that resemble spaghetti.

Riccine are short curled lengths, often ribbed.

Rotelle are wheels or corkscrew lengths.

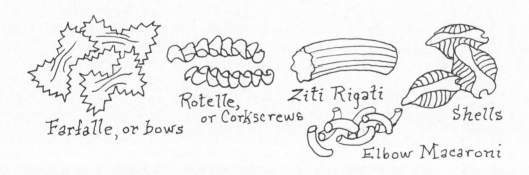

Farfalle, or bows

Rotelle, or Corkscrews

Ziti Rigati

Elbow Macaroni

Shells

COOKING HOMEMADE
AND PACKAGED PASTA

There should be plenty of salted water for pasta to boil in. Two tablespoons of salt in six quarts of water is about the right amount for a pound of spaghetti. For a pound of noodles, some people claim that one tablespoon of salt may be enough. The rule of thumb is to put in one teaspoon of salt for each quart of water, so that three quarts of salted water is considered to be enough for half a pound of pasta. However, we prefer to boil even small amounts of pasta in six quarts of water so that there is plenty of room.

A lid on the pot gets the water boiling faster, of course; the boiling should never stop while the pasta is being added. This is only possible when the pot has a thick bottom and is tall, rather than wide—about nine inches across and almost as deep. Most households have shallower pots of thin metal, so that the water goes off the boil when the pasta is added. This isn't a crucial problem, though, because if boiling stops the lid can be clapped on askew for a moment, until boiling starts again, and no harm done.

Pasta is thrust in the boiling water by the handful. Take a bunch of the stiff strands—about an inch across—and swirl the bundle in the water as if it were a stick, then release as the ends begin to soften. A stir or two with a long fork while the pasta cooks keeps the strands from sticking together, although some people add a few drops of oil to insure against this. Pasta is always cooked with the lid off the pot, because it will boil over if covered.

COOKING TIMES

Times suggested on pasta packages are invariably too long for the ideal firmness called *al dente.* This is the point when there is still some resistance to the bite; no white center should be seen when a strand of spaghetti is bitten into.

Spaghetti may take nine minutes to cook; thinner versions like linguine or spaghettini may be done in six or seven minutes. Homemade noodles may cook in three minutes or less. Packaged noodles may need as much as seven minutes. Noodles generally rise to the surface when cooked, and Italians begin testing for doneness as soon as they rise. A good rule is to begin testing any packaged pasta after it has boiled for five minutes. Children are good testers and are delighted to be asked to judge, although they like softer spaghetti than adults do; they won't eat it if they think it is too firm.

DRAINING

Pasta should not be doused with cold water, as some packages recommend, as this only cools it. Once drained, pasta stops cooking, for all practical purposes. Any powdery flour on the strands comes off in the cooking.

Pasta should be good and moist, so it should not be drained too thoroughly. The strands should be slippery with wetness, and shiny. Some people automatically reserve a cup of the boiling water; in case the pasta is drained too dry, some of the water can be put back on the pasta. Alternately, the pasta can be drained into a colander that has been set in a dish or pan to catch some of the water, so that a tablespoon or so can be put back on the pasta if it has been drained too dry.

SERVING

Pasta should be served at once but it can be kept hot for as long as half an hour. Simply pour the drained pasta back in the emptied cooking pot, stir in a little butter or oil and clap on a lid. The pot can be set in a 200° oven for as long as half an hour and still be acceptable.

Italians insist that pasta can't be reheated; that once cooled, it has to be thrown out. We have found that it warms up perfectly well in a double boiler, when a little hot water, stock or milk is added. Leftover pasta is particularly good with leftover stew, stirred in with it or warmed separately.

PASTA PRONTO

Pasta Pronto

In these quick recipes, the cook is really doing two things at once—making the sauce and cooking the pasta. To keep things simple, the recipes present the steps in making the sauce, indicating where the cooked pasta is incorporated. In most cases, the sauce is made and set to simmer, at which point the pasta is put in salted boiling water, so that the two will be done about the same time. In some cases, the sauce is made while the pasta boils, and kept warm until needed. It is better for the sauce to wait on the pasta; then the other way around. If the sauce takes longer to cook than expected, the pasta can be drained and poured back in the cooking pot with two tablespoons of oil or butter, then tossed gently to coat the strands and set in a warm oven—for as long as half an hour.

Italian cooking is casual, though careful, and there is no call for frenzy. As a reminder, each quick recipe starts off with setting the water for the pasta to boil. A sauce that takes ten minutes or less to make may be started when the water begins to simmer. When the first step of the sauce is done, which might involve cooking an onion in oil until it is soft, the pasta water should be boiling. The cook tosses the pasta into the boiling water and completes the sauce.

The main point is to drain and try to serve the pasta as soon as it is done; its hotness warms up a cooled sauce nicely.

43

Fettuccine al Burro
Noodles with Butter

for 4–6   5 MINUTES

¼ pound butter... equals

1 cup

½ cup... equals

8 tablespoons

Thin egg noodles less than half an inch wide are favorites all
over Italy and are called tagliatelle, except in Rome, where they
are called fettuccine. They won international fame at the hands
of Alfredo di Lelio, who was given a golden spoon and fork by
Mary Pickford and Douglas Fairbanks for tossing his Fettuccine
Alfredo.

Fettuccine Alfredo calls for equal amounts of freshly made
noodles, fresh sweet butter, and freshly grated, aged Parmesan

44

cheese—a pound of each. Alfredo's performance began by slicing large pieces of butter into a hot chafing dish, pouring in the slightly drained fettuccine, slicing in more butter, tossing gently, grating in some Parmesan, tossing to incorporate plenty of air, and so on, until all the butter and cheese was used up. Sometimes, a little of the hot water in which the noodles had cooked was added to keep the hot mass moist, or ¼ cup of heavy cream . . . . It was a meal in itself, perhaps with a little salad and Zabaglione (page 184) for dessert.

Everybody has a personal version of Fettuccine al Burro, even when they call the noodles tagliatelle, and the version as here uses less butter and cheese to gain lightness. The most common addition is parsley; our version also adds basil, giving it the right to be called parsley sauce or even basil sauce. A virtue of any version of Fettuccini al Burro is that it goes well with light red wines like Bardolino, Valpolicella, and the California Gamay Beaujolais, or light white wines like Soave and Frascati. Serve Fettuccine al Burro as a main course with green salad; if a first course is desired, melon and prosciutto would be delicious. Fettuccine also makes an excellent first course or side dish with cold roast beef slices or Chicken with Parsley (page 152).

THE PASTA

Thin noodles. These will cook quickly (especially if homemade)—sometimes in two or three minutes. Romans like fettuccine bitey—just barely *al dente,* or firm to the teeth.

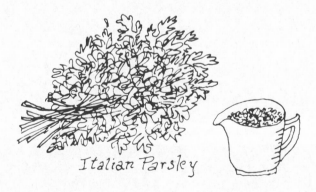

Italian Parsley

SET 6 QUARTS OF WATER TO BOIL, WITH 2 TABLESPOONS SALT; THIS MAY TAKE HALF AN HOUR.

1 POUND FETTUCCINE

ADD THE FETTUCINE TO BOILING WATER AND COOK 4-5 MINUTES, STIRRING OCCASIONALLY, UNTIL NOODLES RISE TO SURFACE OR ARE JUST DONE AND STILL *AL DENTE*, OR FIRM TO THE TOOTH.

½ pound unsalted (sweet) butter
1 cup chopped fresh parsley
2 tablespoons chopped fresh basil, or 1 teaspoon dried
½ teaspoon salt
¼ teaspoon freshly ground pepper

The secret of the excellence of this sauce is fresh unsalted butter and fresh herbs. Italian parsley is to be preferred to the usual curly kind. Use scant measures if dried basil must be used. The final dish may call for more salt and pepper, along with more grated cheese, to be added by the guests.

1 cup Parmesan cheese, at least two years old, freshly grated

Slice some of the butter into a warm bowl or chafing dish and add the seasonings. (See Note.) Drain the noodles quickly, pour into the bowl, slice in the remaining butter. Toss gently, turning the noodles over the melting butter. Sprinkle over some of the cheese and toss again, continuing until all the cheese is incorporated. (Some of the cooking water or ¼ cup of milk or cream may be added for more moistness.)

VARIATIONS

—Add 2 tablespoons of capers just before adding cheese.

—Add ½ cup chopped green or black olives with the herbs.

—Add a 2-ounce can of anchovies, drained and chopped, with the herbs.

—Sprinkle with 2 tablespoons of chopped pimientos or diced green peppers just before serving.

—Cream a stick of softened butter (¼ pound) and gradually beat in 4 tablespoons (¼ cup) of heavy cream, then slowly add ½ cup of freshly grated Parmesan cheese. Toss gently with noodles, and serve with more grated cheese on the side. (A piece of cheese just about doubles in bulk when grated; that is, 2 ounces produces about one-half cup of grated cheese.) Plenty of freshly ground pepper and more butter may be desired. This is an excellent sauce for hot vegetables.

NOTE

A clove or two of garlic is often mashed and simmered for a minute or two with the butter, then removed. Frequently, a combination of oil and butter is used, particularly when additions other than parsley or fresh basil are added, and when something less than the freshest country butter, or when salted butter, is used.

Aglio e Olio
Garlic and Oil Sauce

for 4–6   5 MINUTES

When the freshest butter for spaghetti isn't available, the cook is apt to settle for oil and garlic, particularly if he is from the south. Sometimes, the garlic is thinly sliced and simmered in the oil until transparent; other times, it is mashed and slightly browned; still other times, it is crushed slightly and pressed in the heating oil with a spoon and then removed. But the preferred way seems to be to chop the cloves; more or less finely, let them become lightly golden in the oil, then quickly add something else—usually parsley or fresh basil in the spring, oregano during the summer.

The Neapolitan way is simply to warm chopped garlic in the oil, then pour it over the spaghetti and toss. Gently. Two or three cloves of garlic per person are used instead of the single clove for each person called for here. No cheese is served. Aglio e Olio is good with any red or white wine but best with the crisp dry whites of Ischia or Capri or The California Grey Riesling. Served as a first course, Aglio e Olio could be followed by some freshly caught pan-fried fish, a green salad, and cheese, then strawberries with Marsala. This is best followed by a siesta.

THE PASTA
Spaghetti or thinner spaghettini or vermicelli are used most.

48

SET 6 QUARTS OF WATER TO BOIL, WITH 2 TABLESPOONS OF SALT; THIS MAY TAKE HALF AN HOUR.

1 POUND SPAGHETTI

ADD THE SPAGHETTI TO BOILING WATER AND COOK 8–9 MINUTES, OR UNTIL SPAGHETTI IS JUST DONE, BUT STILL FIRM TO THE BITE.

1 cup olive oil
4 garlic cloves, chopped
½ cup chopped fresh parsley
1 teaspoon dried oregano
   or basil (optional)
½ teaspoon salt
¼ teaspoon pepper,
   freshly ground

Warm oil in small saucepan or skillet, but not too hot. Add the garlic, parsley, oregano, and seasonings to the warm oil and let steep 2–3 minutes. Do not let garlic brown.

Drain spaghetti, then pour into warm bowl, pour sauce over, and toss gently.

VARIATIONS

—Stir into the hot oil a two-ounce can of anchovies, drained, and simmer for 2–3 minutes before adding garlic. Omit the salt.

—Add a small chili pepper, called *peperoncino*, with the garlic, and then remove; or sprinkle in a few flakes of dried red pepper.

—Before adding garlic, simmer a small sliced onion in the oil, along with ¼ cup of vinegar. (This version, halved, is an excellent green sauce for cooked vegetables, as well as for pasta.)

NOTE

As much as half a cup of butter is often substituted for part of the oil; or 2 tablespoons of butter is put in the bottom of the warm bowl before the spaghetti is put in; or a tablespoon of butter is added to each portion.

Sauce Ramatuelle

for 4–6   3 MINUTES

This simple dish of fresh basil and raw tomatoes with garlic mashed in salt, over which spaghetti is poured and tossed, was discovered during a summer spent in a pokey little resort near swinging St. Tropez. It is the lightest pasta dish we have ever tasted.

Since then, we have discovered a version from the island of Ischia, Capri's neighbor, that calls for a squeeze of lemon, and a version of *that* calling for scallions and chopped parsley in place of the basil. These versions are delicious with white wines from the above two islands, but Ramatuelle is also good with the light French reds of Provence, like Bandol or Bellet; the rosés of Cassis; and a light red from California like Ruby Cabernet. This dish is a meal in itself, preceded by salami and other sausages, followed by salad, cheese, and Pears in Red Wine (page 187). It is also spectacular as a first course before a broiled fish.

Sauce Ramatuelle is meant to be varied freely. First love's best, however, and we prefer it just as we found it, without a grating of cheese. It is our favorite summer dish.

THE PASTA
Spaghettini, or any thin pasta.

½ cup olive oil
3 large ripe tomatoes, chopped
3 cloves garlic
3 teaspoons salt

SET 6 QUARTS OF WATER TO BOIL, WITH 2 TABLESPOONS OF SALT; THIS MAY TAKE HALF AN HOUR.

Pour the olive oil into a large serving bowl and add the chopped tomatoes. Mash the garlic with the salt and put it in

50

1 cup chopped fresh basil
  leaves
¼ teaspoon pepper,
  freshly ground
1 POUND SPAGHETTINI

the bowl. Tear the basil leaves into con-
fetti-sized bits, or chop coarsely. Add the
pepper.

PUT THE SPAGHETTINI INTO BOILING WA-
TER AND COOK 7–8 MINUTES, OR UNTIL
JUST DONE AND STILL FIRM.

Drain the hot spaghettini and dump into
the bowl. Toss thoroughly and serve immediately.

VARIATIONS

—Rub the bowl with a hot red pepper before pouring in the oil.
For real hotness, add a small hot pepper, chopped finely, to the
sauce. The chopped pepper can be served in a side dish, or can
be put in a cruet that is then filled with olive oil, a few drops of
which the guest can add to his serving. The peppery oil can be
replenished indefinitely, a tablespoon at a time, and can be used
on any dish where peppery hotness is wanted.

—Add chopped green peppers and black olives, perhaps ¼ cup
of each.

—Three or four mashed anchovies can be substituted for the salt.

—Add raw mushrooms, about ¼ pound, thinly sliced.

—Strips of sautéed eggplant can be added.

—Add as much as a cup of cooked chicken or veal or tongue,
cut julienne (an eighth of an inch thick and a quarter of an inch
wide).

—Add a cupful of boiled shrimp, chopped, or some cooked fish,
or crabmeat.

—Instead of fresh basil, ½ cup fresh, chopped parsley and 1 teaspoon dried basil could be used.

51

Il Pesto
Basil Sauce

for 4–6　　　　　　　　　　　　　　　　　10 MINUTES

Il Pesto, named after the sauce, is considered the greatest of all
pasta dishes. A specialty of Genoa, the local matchstick noodle
called trenette is traditionally used for it, but the sauce is delicious on various noodles and thin spaghettis. Il Pesto must be
made with fresh basil from the countryside, say the Genoese, anything else being too bitter. This is local pride. Pine nuts are considered essential, too, but walnuts or almonds are a perfectly ac-

ceptable substitute; and it is delicious with no nuts at all. The Genoese insist on using grated Sardo cheese combined with Pecorino Romano, but Parmesan cheese is excellent.

The preferred way of making Il Pesto is to crush the ingredients in a mortar, adding olive oil slowly to make a thick paste, pleasingly lumpy. It can be made equally well in a blender, the result being like thick cream. Some recipes omit parsley, but a cupful is essential for a good version that calls for a teaspoonful of dried basil moistened in a tablespoonful of hot water, (this isn't a bit like the fresh basil, however). The sauce keeps for weeks in the refrigerator if covered with a thin coating of olive oil and sealed tightly. So they can have it all winter, many people make batches of Il Pesto with the last of the basil in the fall, freezing just the basil and the oil. The rest of the ingredients can be added later. A spoonful is good in soups or on grilled steaks.

When serving, a great tablespoonful of Il Pesto is put on each plate of trenette, along with a tablespoon of soft butter and a grating of cheese. As a first course, it can precede any dish, particularly roasts. As a main course, it might be preceded or followed by servings of prosciutto or salami with black olives; salad, cheese, and fruit for dessert complete a satisfying and novel meal. Red wine is customary, a full Barolo, a fruity Chianti, or the New York Baco Noir.

THE PASTA
Trenette or any thin noodle like fettuccine or linguine, even spaghettini, is excellent with Il Pesto.

SET 6 QUARTS WATER TO BOIL, WITH 2 TABLESPOONS SALT; THIS MAY TAKE HALF AN HOUR.

53

PASTA PRONTO!

1 cup fresh basil, tightly
packed

½ cup fresh parsley (Italian,
if possible), tightly packed

3 cloves garlic, chopped

¼ cup pine nuts and/or
walnuts or almonds

½ cup grated Sardo and/or
Pecorino Romano cheese

¼ teaspoon salt

½ cup olive oil

Place the ingredients listed ahead of the olive oil in a blender or mortar, and blend or pound to a paste. (Add a tablespoon of the olive oil if the blender does not grind everything thoroughly.)

Add the olive oil in dribbles, a teaspoonful at a time, until the mixture is the consistency of thick cream.

1 POUND TRENETTE

PUT NOODLES IN THE BOILING WATER AND COOK 5–6 MINUTES, OR UNTIL DONE BUT STILL FIRM.

¼ pound butter, softened

½ cup grated Parmesan, Sardo,
or Pecorino Romano cheese

Drain noodles and serve individual portions with a generous tablespoonful of butter and at least an equal amount of sauce. Serve the rest of the sauce on the side, with a bowl of the Parmesan cheese.

VARIATIONS

—A quarter of a teaspoon of freshly ground pepper or red pepper flakes may be added to the sauce.

—A cup of fresh spinach may be substituted for the basil.

NOTE

Proportions may be varied freely—the amount of cheese may be doubled or the oil reduced by half, for instance—but the aim is to produce a hearty sauce that is muted by the butter and the blandness of the noodles.

Pasta con Tre Formaggi
Pasta with Three Cheeses

for 4–6   5 MINUTES

Cheese and pasta are such boon companions that there are a group of sauces, all rich, that consist of nothing else—except butter and milk or cream, of course, and salt and pepper. They make a repertoire of dishes, all by themselves.

The blandest cheese-and-pasta recipe calls for a cupful each of butter and cream cheese (the Italians call it mascarpone) tossed with the pasta in a hot pan or chafing dish. The two can be cut into the hot pasta or creamed together with a tablespoonful or so of the hot water in which the pasta is cooking.

A slightly tastier recipe is made with a cupful of ricotta, the smooth Italian version of cottage cheese, beaten to creaminess and combined with half cupfuls of grated Parmesan and butter. This can also be made with cottage cheese that has been stirred to smoothness with a tablespoonful or so of cream. As first

55

courses, these dishes are fine to serve before slices of cold roast beef or chicken. They are also good accompaniments for baked ham, roasts, or spicy veal birds, but they need a crumble of bacon or a generous sprinkling of prosciutto or dried beef or a julienne of tongue to be satisfying as a main dish.

A more assertive recipe combines a hard grating cheese like aged Parmesan or Sardo, a mild cheese like fontina or Gruyère, and a soft cheese like mozzarella. Pasta con Tre Formaggi makes a marvelous main-course dish, plain or enhanced by ham or bacon.

The simplicity of such a three-cheese sauce, without adornment, calls for a crisp or flavorsome first course—like antipasto or sautéed shrimp—a crisp salad, and a sharp dessert—like sliced oranges with anisette. Most of all, it calls for wine, plenty of light reds like Bardolino or Valpolicella or California Zinfandel. With black coffee, serve anise-flavored cookies and grappa.

THE PASTA

Spaghetti or thinner spaghettini, thin noodles like tagliatelle or fettuccine, or linguine, can be used.

1 POUND SPAGHETTI

SET 6 QUARTS OF WATER TO BOIL, WITH 2 TABLESPOONS SALT; THIS MAY TAKE HALF AN HOUR. PUT 1 POUND SPAGHETTI IN BOILING WATER AND COOK 7–8 MINUTES OR UNTIL DONE, BUT STILL FIRM.

½ cup melted butter
½ teaspoon salt
¼ teaspoon pepper
   freshly ground
3 ounces mozzarella, sliced,
   about ⅔ cup

Pour half the butter into a warm chafing dish or an electric skillet set to warm. (Reserve ½ cup of the cooking water.) Drain the spaghetti and pour it into the dish or skillet. Add the salt and pepper and mozzarella, and toss until the cheese is almost melted.

3 ounces Gruyère or
Emmenthaler, grated

3 ounces Parmesan or Romano,
grated

½ cup hot milk or
½ cup cooking water from
the spaghetti (optional)

Add the Gruyère, toss lightly; add the rest of the butter and toss until the cheese is almost melted.

Add the Parmesan and toss again. If the spaghetti is too dry, add some of the hot milk, or some of the cooking water, until the spaghetti has a creamy look. Serve at once.

VARIATIONS

—Add half a cup of ricotta at the end, beaten until fluffy with two tablespoons of the cooking water.

—Add ½ cup of cream or sour cream at the end, tossing gently until the spaghetti is thoroughly hot again.

—Add as much as one cup of smoked meats—ham, dried beef sausages like hard salami or bologna, or crisp bacon.

—Stir in at the end ¼ pound of mushrooms that have been thinly sliced and sautéed in 2 tablespoons of butter.

—Scatter over each serving 6–8 slices of olives, green or black.

—Sprinkle over each serving a spoonful of croutons, made by cutting bread into ½-inch cubes, enough to make a cupful, and sautéeing them until golden in 2 tablespoons each of butter and olive oil.

—Edam or Gouda, Tilsit or Münster, can be substituted for one of the cheeses—preferably the mozzarella.

—Sharp Cheddar or fontina can replace the Gruyère. Any Italian grating cheese can be used.

Green Velvet Sauce

for 4–6   10 MINUTES

This is a simple and subtle sauce, perhaps the most interesting of parsley sauces, contrived by a Russian lady who lives in New York and entertains with this dish whenever she can muster the strength to chop all the parsley. She does it with a mezzaluna, the half-moon chopping knife that is in every Italian kitchen. She claims the sauce is not as good when done in a blender. She is also fussy about the garlic, mashing it under the blade of a knife with a smart blow, then chopping it still finer, so that the shreds are well broken up. She not only serves the sauce with pasta, but also adds a spoonful or so to a risotto, puts a dollop on steaks and chops, serves it over cold poached salmon.

Pasta with Green Velvet Sauce is an excellent first course, served with thin breadsticks, *grissini,* and plenty of red wine, like a Gattinara or Lambrusco; then roast or barbecued chicken would be an excellent main course. Green Velvet Sauce is almost too subtle for a main course, unless preceded by a lavish antipasto and accompanied by cold slices of rare roast beef and a salad of endive, black olives, and sliced oranges. The meal ends with Pears with Marsala, (page 186), Strega, and espresso.

Green Velvet Sauce can be made ahead of time and refrigerated. Just be sure to serve at room temperature.

THE PASTA
Spaghetti, spaghettini, or vermicelli.

SET 6 QUARTS OF WATER TO BOIL, WITH
2 TABLESPOONS SALT; THIS MAY TAKE
HALF AN HOUR.

4 slices bread, crusts removed
¼ cup wine vinegar

Pile the trimmed slices of bread in a small bowl and pour the vinegar over them. Turn them and see that they are thoroughly soaked.

2 cups parsley, preferably
   Italian, very finely chopped
4 garlic cloves, mashed and
   finely minced
½ teaspoon salt, or more
¼ teaspoon freshly ground
   black pepper, or more
¾ cup olive oil

Chop the parsley as finely as possible (see Note), and place in a mixing bowl. Squeeze the bread dry, and break up into bits. Add to the parsley. Mix thoroughly; add the garlic and seasonings and mix again. Beat in the oil, a little at a time. Beat until smooth and thick. Check seasoning, adding more salt and pepper to taste.

1 POUND SPAGHETTI

PUT SPAGHETTI IN BOILING WATER AND COOK 7–8 MINUTES OR UNTIL DONE, BUT STILL FIRM.

1 hard-cooked egg, chopped

Serve sauce in a bowl, with the chopped egg sprinkled on it, to use on well-buttered spaghetti.

NOTE

Green Velvet Sauce can be made in a blender. If you do use a blender, use 4 cups of parsley, chopped coarsely instead of finely. Blend ingredients until smooth and bright green.

Linguine con Salsa di Vongole, Bianca
Spaghetti with White Clam Sauce

for 4–6   5 MINUTES

Clam sauce is the most popular of all those using seafood and is served as a white sauce or a red one, with or without tomatoes. The white sauce is perhaps more distinctive, particularly when served with a chilled dry white wine like Verdicchio, Orvieto, or California Chardonnay. Clam sauce is generally served over the thin oval spaghetti called linguine. Some cooks insist it should be served with grated Pecorino Romano, while others are vehement about omitting the cheese entirely.

Canned clams produce an excellent sauce. Fresh clams, oysters, or mussels can be used, removed from their shells, with the liquid reserved and strained for use in the sauce. A couple of dozen fresh clams is enough for four people, although twice as many is not too much; a pint of fresh clams bought without their shells is sufficient. With fresh clams the hard parts should be minced, the soft parts chopped (the hard part can be felt with the fingers).

This is a perfect luncheon dish, followed by salad and cheese. For dinner it is a fine first course to precede grilled or sautéed fish and sliced tomatoes. An excellent dessert is one that calls for lemon—a sherbet, slices of melon, or a fruit cup.

THE PASTA
Linguine, vermicelli, or spaghettini.

60

SET 6 QUARTS WATER TO BOIL, WITH 2 TABLESPOONS SALT; THIS MAY TAKE HALF AN HOUR.

1 POUND LINGUINE

ADD LINGUINE AND COOK 5–6 MINUTES OR UNTIL DONE BUT STILL FIRM.

½ cup olive oil
3 cloves garlic, mashed
2 7-ounce cans minced clams,
   or 2–3 dozen fresh clams,
   or 1 pint shucked clams
¼ teaspoon freshly ground
   black pepper
½ cup finely chopped fresh
   parsley

2 tablespoons butter
1 cup freshly grated Parmesan
   cheese

Clams should not overcook, so this sauce can be started after the linguine goes into the boiling water.

Heat the oil in a skillet and add the garlic, cooking until soft. (The garlic may be left in or removed.) Add the clams and their strained juice, the pepper, and half the parsley. Bring just to a simmer.

Drain linguine, pour into a hot bowl, and toss with the butter. Serve the sauce on individual servings, sprinkled with the rest of the parsley, and cheese offered in a bowl.

VARIATIONS

—Add ½ teaspoon dried basil and/or thyme when clams are added, or a teaspoonful of the fresh herbs when available.

—Add ¼ teaspoon dried oregano or red pepper flakes with the clams.

—Squeeze the juice of half a lemon over the clam sauce just before it is removed from the heat.

Vermicelli con Vongole, Salsa Rossa

Spaghetti with Red Clam Sauce

for 4–6   20 MINUTES

Shucked raw clams poached in olive oil and tomatoes is one of the seacoast wonders of the world, varying slightly from place to place, but perhaps best in Naples. There, the clams are often steamed first, in a covered pan with about one-fourth cup of olive oil into which a garlic clove has been pressed for a minute, but sometimes in half a cup of wine. If shucking clams is a nuisance, steaming them first is the easier way; they are simply added to the hot sauce. In either case, the juice is strained before being added to the sauce. When baby clams or mussels are used, there seems scarcely any need for mincing them.

Spaghetti with red clam sauce is an excellent first course before a grilled steak or a plate of cold cuts, served with plenty of rough red wine like a Chianti in its straw-covered *fiasco,* a Côte du Rhone from France, a Barbera, or a Petite Syrah from California. It can be a meal in itself when served with a platter of corn on the cob, a tossed green salad, crusty bread, and cheese, with watermelon for dessert. No cheese would be served with the clam sauce.

THE PASTA

Thin spaghetti like vermicelli or linguine is used most.

62

SET 6 QUARTS WATER TO BOIL, WITH 2 TABLESPOONS SALT; THIS MAY TAKE HALF AN HOUR.

½ cup olive oil
2 cloves garlic, split
3–4 tomatoes, peeled and
  seeded, or 2 cups canned
  Italian plum tomatoes, sieved

Heat the oil in a large skillet, add the garlic slivers, and cook until they are golden; then remove them. Add the tomatoes and simmer for 15 minutes, or until sauce thickens.

1 POUND VERMICELLI

PUT VERMICELLI IN THE BOILING WATER AND COOK 4–5 MINUTES, OR UNTIL DONE, BUT STILL FIRM.

2 7-ounce cans minced clams,
  or 2–3 dozen fresh clams,
  or 1 pint shucked clams
¼ teaspoon freshly ground
  black pepper
½ cup finely chopped fresh
  parsley

Add the strained juice from the clams, stirring it through the sauce. Add the clams and pepper, and bring to a simmer.

Drain the vermicelli and turn into a hot bowl. Add the sauce and toss gently. Serve at once, sprinkling parsley over each serving.

VARIATIONS
—Use mussels instead of clams.

Vermicelli con Acciughe
Spaghetti with Anchovies

for 4   10 MINUTES

This is one of the most delicious ways to eat pasta. Much of the saltiness of the anchovies is lost to the spaghetti. The flavor of the fish combines perfectly with whatever else one chooses to add—olives, perhaps, or as much as a tablespoon of capers and some mint, or a julienne of cooked pork, veal, or chicken is

64

wonderful, sprinkled on top. Spaghetti and anchovies is a good first course before grilled fish or a steak, a good main course when followed by a big salad. White wines like Soave or Frascati or California Chenin Blanc are excellent. A light and cool dessert like Biscuit Tortoni (page 183) or chilled fruit and coffee with brandy completes the meal.

Anchovies packed in salt need rinsing, but that is not called for with anchovies canned in oil, the kind most readily available; there is no need to drain the anchovies because a good quality of oil is used for packing the top brands. The fillets dissolve almost instantly when simmered. Reserve a few, chopped or whole, to garnish each serving. Tossing should be thorough so that the dissolved anchovy coats the spaghetti evenly. Salt is not likely to be needed. Guests can grate black pepper on their own servings, and may or may not add some grated Pecorino Romano or Parmesan. This recipe makes a small amount of sauce, but it is quite enough for a pound of spaghetti; doubting cooks might double the amount of olive oil.

THE PASTA
Any spaghetti will do, from thin vermicelli to thicker pasta; thin macaroni and bucatini is often used.

SET 6 QUARTS WATER TO BOIL, WITH 2 TABLESPOONS SALT; THIS MAY TAKE HALF AN HOUR.

½ cup butter
½ cup olive oil
4 garlic cloves, finely chopped
2 2-ounce cans anchovy fillets
12–24 black olives, chopped

Melt the butter with the oil in a skillet, add the garlic and cook until soft. (All or part of the garlic can be discarded at this point, but it is often left in.) Add anchovies to simmering oil, stirring for 2 minutes, until they dissolve. (Reserve 4–6 fillets for garnish.) Add olives and stir. Keep sauce warm.

PASTA PRONTO!

1 POUND VERMICELLI

COOK VERMICELLI IN BOILING WATER 4–5 MINUTES, OR UNTIL DONE, BUT STILL FIRM.

¼ cup chopped parsley

Drain vermicelli and pour into warm bowl. Add sauce and toss thoroughly. Sprinkle with parsley and reserved anchovies, chopped or whole, and serve. (Reserved anchovies may be stirred into the sauce at the last minute to mute their flavor.)

VARIATIONS

—Add 1 teaspoon chopped fresh oregano, or ½ teaspoon dried, with the olives.

—Add 1 tablespoon capers and 1 teaspoon chopped fresh mint with the olives.

—Add a small chopped green pepper with the anchovies.

—Add 3–4 dried Italian mushrooms that have been soaked in ½ cup hot water for 10 minutes, then chopped, after the anchovies have dissolved.

—Add a 7-ounce can of tuna fish (drained if not packed in oil) after the anchovies have dissolved.

NOTE

The famous Piedmontese sauce, Bagna Cauda (page 171), used as a dip for raw vegetables, can be made by halving the oil and using a single can of anchovies. The hot bath is usually served in the small pan it is cooked in, kept hot over a candle warmer. The parsley and olives are left out, but thin slices of white truffle are often added.

Spaghetti alla Salsa di Tonno
Spaghetti with Tuna Sauce

for 4–6   10 MINUTES

Italians do marvels with tuna and other canned or smoked fish, adding various things with the greatest nonchalance, then coming forth with a steaming bowl of spaghetti of bewildering goodness. Preparation seems to be nothing more than chopping some parsley for garnish, warming up a can of tuna in some butter, and adding something—a little bouillon, or a cup of warmed cream or leftover sauce, some anchovies and a tablespoonful of capers, or a handful of olives. The basic white tuna sauce is a repertoire.

So is the red tuna sauce, given here, which includes tomatoes, and maybe some mushrooms or peas or ham. The tuna may go in early, so that it will disintegrate with a little stirring; or added later, so that chunks will remain.

As a main course, two cans of tuna might be used, preceded by Caponata (page 172). As a first course, only one can would be incorporated, followed by a chicken or veal dish, or a grilled meat. In any case, a light red wine like a Bardolino or California Gamay, or a chilled white wine like Verdicchio or California Johannisberg Riesling, can be served. After cheese and salad, a pleasing dessert is orange slices sprinkled with sugar and steeped for an hour in a couple of tablespoons of kirsch, followed by grappa and espresso.

THE PASTA
Any spaghetti, thick or thin.

67

SET 6 QUARTS WATER TO BOIL, WITH 2 TABLESPOONS SALT; THIS MAY TAKE HALF AN HOUR.

2 tablespoons butter
1 garlic clove, chopped
2 anchovy fillets
    (optional)
¼ pound fresh mushrooms,
    sliced (See Note.)
1 7-ounce can of Italian
    tuna, packed in oil
½ cup canned tomato sauce
¼ teaspoon freshly grated
    pepper
½ teaspoon salt (or less)

Melt butter in a saucepan and cook garlic until soft. Discard, if desired. Add the anchovies and stir until they begin to dissolve, then add the mushrooms and cook until soft. Add the tuna and warm; or simmer and stir until the tuna fish is broken up and almost dissolved.

1 POUND SPAGHETTI

COOK SPAGHETTI IN BOILING WATER 7–8 MINUTES, OR UNTIL DONE, BUT STILL FIRM.

Add tomato sauce to sauce and simmer 5 minutes, or until spaghetti is done.

¼ cup chopped parsley

Drain spaghetti and turn into warm bowl, pour sauce over, and toss gently. Garnish with parsley and serve.

Correct seasoning; no added salt may be needed if anchovies are used.

VARIATIONS

—A cup of fresh tomatoes, peeled, seeded, and chopped, or a cup of canned Italian tomatoes, sieved, can be substituted for tomato sauce. Cook for 10 minutes before tuna is added.

—A cup of cooked peas can be added at the last minute, in place of the mushrooms. A sliced onion sautéed with the garlic might be added, in this case.

—A chopped green pepper, or thin slices, or pieces an inch square, can be sautéed with the garlic.

—2 tablespoons of chopped chives can be added at the last minute, omitting the garlic.

NOTE

Dried Italian mushrooms add a distinctive taste. They come in half-ounce packages, and need to be soaked in ½ cup of hot water for 5 minutes to be reconstituted. They are then drained and chopped, the water being added to the tomatoes.

The Roman version of tuna sauce, *alla carretiere*, calls for cooking the garlic, parsley, dried mushrooms, and tuna in its oil, adding an ounce of white wine and letting it reduce, then adding the tomato sauce, salt, and pepper, and simmering for half an hour. This "coachman's way" can be made without adding the dollop of wine, but it is better with it.

Spaghetti à la Môde de Grand Mère

Spaghetti, Grandmother's Style

for 4–6   10 MINUTES

The Swiss have adopted many Italian pasta dishes, but this one seems to be their own invention. It has become part of the international cuisine. The buttery croutons, ham, and bacon are a pleasing collection of textures with spaghetti.

This is an excellent first course to serve before a simply broiled chicken or fish, and it is also good before main courses that are bland or are served with cream sauces. As a main course for luncheon, it is delicious with an omelet. By itself, it might be preceded by anything served with mayonnaise, from hard-boiled eggs to cold poached fish or seafood. A light green salad and cheese might follow it, with a dessert like pears poached in Marsala (page 186). It seems to call for light white wines—a Soave or Verdicchio, a California Riesling or Folle Blanche, a New York or California Geürztraminer.

THE PASTA
Any spaghetti, or thin noodles.

SET 6 QUARTS WATER TO BOIL, WITH 2 TABLESPOONS SALT; THIS MAY TAKE HALF AN HOUR.

2 slices bacon, at least
    ¼ inch thick, diced
6 ounces cooked ham, cut in
    ½ inch cubes
3 slices bread, cut in
    ½ inch cubes
1 tablespoon butter, or more
1 tablespoon olive oil, or more

In a large skillet, slowly cook the bacon with the ham, until the bacon is crisp. Remove with a slotted spoon and drain on paper towel.

Add the butter and oil to the fat in the pan, and when the foam has subsided, turn up the heat slightly and add the bread cubes. Stir until slightly brown on all sides, adding more butter and oil, if necessary. Remove with slotted spoon and drain on paper towel.

1 POUND SPAGHETTI

PUT SPAGHETTI IN BOILING WATER AND COOK 8–9 MINUTES, OR UNTIL DONE, BUT STILL FIRM.

2 ounces Parmesan cheese,
    grated
4 tablespoons butter
¼ teaspoon pepper

Drain spaghetti and dump into warm bowl. Toss with butter and pepper. Add ham, bacon, and croutons and toss gently. Add more butter, if necessary. Serve grated cheese on the side.

71

Spaghettini all' Amatriciana
Spaghettini, Amatrice Style

for 4–6   20 MINUTES

A true Roman is one who comes from seven generations of Romans. This recipe, a Roman classic, comes from one whose grandmother was a true Roman but whose grandfather was a Venetian. It originated in the Roman hill town of Amatrice, where linguine and lard and pork cheek are traditional ingredients. Venetian liberality condones the substitution of bacon or salt pork.

L'Amatriciana varies according to the way the salt pork is cut, the taste seeming to vary from small to large dice. The most typical way is to cut slices about an eighth inch thick, half an inch wide, and less than two inches long; a four-ounce block of salt pork is enough for a pound of pasta, making about ¾ cup when sliced. Fresh tomatoes are an acceptable addition.

Some recipes call for adding half a cup of white wine after the onion has gone limp, then letting this reduce, but the step is frequently omitted. Plenty of freshly ground pepper is essential. Grated Pecorino Romano cheese is preferred to Parmesan, although some Romans use both. The salt pork may be removed when golden, then sprinkled over each serving at the end, but often enough it is left to cook with the sauce. The recipe can be quite meticulous, although it should not be at all surprising that every Roman has his own way of making the dish just so, praising loudly any version served but secretly believing that his own is a little better.

With drinks before dinner, black olives with oranges (page 176) are delicious. This is a hearty pasta dish, and first-course servings should be small. Grilled steaks or chops that follow would receive a squeeze of lemon before being served. Sprightly red wines like Chianti, Nebbiolo, and Barbera from California, are good with both courses, followed by a salad of fennel or rocket with other greens. Pears or apples with cheese are traditional desserts. Espresso might be served with Italian brandy or grappa, or anise liqueur like the one called Mistra.

THE PASTA
Spaghettini, linguine, or thin macaroni like bucatini.

SET 6 QUARTS WATER TO BOIL, WITH 2 TABLESPOONS SALT; THIS MAY TAKE HALF AN HOUR.

73

⅔–¾ cup olive oil
1 medium onion, sliced

4 ounces salt pork or
4–6 slices bacon,
cut in slices about
⅛ inch thick, ½ inch
wide and 1½ inches long
1 can (2 pounds 3 ounces)
Italian plum tomatoes,
drained, or 2–3 pounds
fresh tomatoes, seeded
and chopped
½ teaspoon salt, or less
½ teaspoon freshly
ground black pepper

Heat olive oil in skillet, add onions and stir until they are just transparent. Add salt pork and cook until it is just golden. (Romans sometimes remove the salt pork and sprinkle it over the dish just before serving.)

Add the drained tomatoes and simmer over low heat for 10 minutes. They should cook until all the water evaporates, but should not lose their shape.

1 POUND SPAGHETTINI

PUT SPAGHETTINI IN BOILING WATER AND COOK 8–9 MINUTES, OR UNTIL DONE, BUT STILL FIRM.

4 ounces Pecorino
Romano, freshly
grated

Taste for saltiness; no additional salt may be needed. Add pepper.

Drain spaghettini—but not too thoroughly—pour in a warmed bowl, add the sauce, and toss gently but completely. Add half the cheese and toss again, serving remainder in a side dish. (If salt pork has been removed, strew over spaghettini and serve.)

74

Trenette alla Carbonara
Noodles, Woodcutter's Way

for 4–6   10 MINUTES

La Carbonara is one of the glories of Rome, rarely good in restaurants outside Italy because it must be served very hot, and only Romans seem to care enough to make it properly. An egg or two is broken into the hot spaghetti and then tossed thoroughly so that the pasta becomes richly yellow. Salt pork is particularly delicious in this dish, but lean regular bacon or Canadian bacon are good substitutes.

This is an excellent dish to make in a chafing dish over a low flame, or over a candle warmer, the spaghetti being tossed with the egg and cheese, then the sizzling salt pork or bacon being added for a final tossing. Serve with a crisp salad with oil and lemon dressing and wines either white or red—Frascati, Verdicchio, Chianti, Bardolino, or the California Chenin Blanc. A first course might be Caponata (page 172). Fresh fruit is a perfect dessert, with Strega or Fior d'Alpi and espresso.

75

PASTA PRONTO!

THE PASTA

The trenette pasta of Genoa seems to take up slightly more of the sauce than linguine or spaghetti, and is recommended because of that happy characteristic.

SET 6 QUARTS WATER TO BOIL, WITH 2 TABLESPOONS SALT; THIS MAY TAKE HALF AN HOUR.

1 POUND TRENETTE

PUT TRENETTE IN BOILING WATER AND COOK 5–6 MINUTES, OR UNTIL DONE, BUT STILL FIRM.

½ cup butter or lard
4 ounces lean salt pork,
    diced, or 6 slices lean
    bacon, diced

Melt the butter in a small skillet over medium heat and add the salt pork. Cook until lightly golden here and there.

2 eggs, lightly beaten

4 ounces Pecorino Romano
    or Parmesan, freshly grated
½ teaspoon freshly ground
    pepper

2–3 tablespoons milk or
    light cream (optional)

Drain trenette and dump into warm bowl or chafing dish. Pour in eggs, toss lightly, and pour in the butter-and-salt-pork mixture. Toss again, add half the cheese, and toss thoroughly. Add the pepper and some more of the cheese. If pasta seems too dry, add the milk, and toss again.

Serve remaining cheese on the side.

VARIATIONS

—The hot pasta can be divided into individual servings on hot plates, forked directly to them from the boiling water. Each guest breaks an egg into the serving, stirring it well, adds cheese and pepper, then pours over all some of the butter-and-salt-pork mixture.

—Just before serving, add a cup of sautéed mushrooms to the pasta.

76

—A couple of Italian sausages, hot or sweet, can replace the salt pork. If sausages are used, sauté them separately before adding to the butter; omit the oil.

—Add ½ cup of the grated Parmesan directly to the beaten eggs.

NOTE

People fret about whether the hot pasta will scramble the eggs. This rarely happens, as long as the pasta is still quite moist when it goes into the bowl. A further precaution is to put a table-spoonful of butter or oil in the bowl before dumping in the pasta, then tossing the pasta enough so that the strands are coated. Some of the milk can also be added at this point.

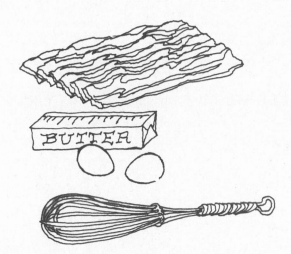

Pasta con Salsicci
Spaghetti with Sausages

for 4–6   20 MINUTES

Sausages, sweet or hot, are Italian specialties. They make a
hearty and appetizing sauce for spaghetti; sometimes they are
browned, but often they are simply stewed with tomatoes or
wine. However they are prepared, the taste of the sausage should
dominate the dish. Here, they are browned so as to impart a certain crispness and to render some of the fat.

Nothing need precede this hearty dish, except perhaps some
raw vegetables with a hot dip—Bagna Cauda (page 171). White
wines like Soave, Verdicchio, and the California Petite Syrah
taste good with the pasta, along with a spinach or Plain Bean
Salad (page 176). Pineapple with kirsch or Pears Poached in Red
Wine (page 187) are refreshing desserts, followed by grappa and
espresso.

THE PASTA
Any spaghetti, thick or thin.

SET 6 QUARTS OF WATER TO BOIL, WITH
2 TABLESPOONS OF SALT; THIS MAY
TAKE HALF AN HOUR.

1 tablespoon dry or sweet
   vermouth, or Marsala
1 pound Italian sausage,
   sweet and/or hot,
   skinned

Put the wine in a skillet and crumble in
the sausage. Cook until lightly browned,
breaking it up with a fork as it cooks
into more or less uniform chunks. Re-

78

1 tablespoon olive oil
1 small onion, chopped
1 garlic clove, crushed
  and minced

1 cup dry white wine or
  ½ cup vermouth with
  ½ cup water

½ cup tomato sauce
the browned sausage

move sausage with a slotted spoon and reserve. Pour off all but one tablespoon of the fat from the pan.

Add olive oil and the onion and garlic, and cook over a low flame until the onion is limp and transparent.

Add the wine and simmer until it has been reduced by half.

Stir in the tomato sauce; add the sausage, cover and simmer for 15 minutes.

1 POUND THIN SPAGHETTI

BEFORE THE SAUCE IS DONE, PUT SPAGHETTI IN BOILING WATER AND COOK 6–7 MINUTES, OR UNTIL DONE, BUT STILL FIRM.

1 tablespoon olive oil

¼ cup fresh parsley,
  chopped
¼ cup grated Romano or
  Parmesan cheese

Drain the spaghetti, reserving 1 cup of cooking water, and turn into a bowl with a tablespoon of olive oil. Add the sauce and toss until thoroughly mixed.

Stir in the parsley and cheese.

For more moistness, add a little more olive oil or a little of the cooking water.

VARIATIONS

—After adding the wine and letting it reduce, add 3 whole canned tomatoes, drained and chopped, instead of the tomato sauce. Cook, with the sausage, for 15 minutes. Add salt to taste.

—Add 1 teaspoon of basil or oregano, or ½ teaspoon of each, to the tomato sauce.

—Add half a green pepper, in thin slivers, with the tomato sauce.

Spaghetti alla Fegatini di Pollo
Spaghetti with Chicken Livers

for 4–6   10 MINUTES

Most spaghetti sauces that cook rapidly can be made in a chafing dish or electric skillet. This one is especially appropriate because it ends in a flicker of flame, which will attract the attention of bemused guests. The trick is to warm the wine or spirit to be flamed—by setting the wine bottle in a small saucepan of hot water or by putting the wine in a saucepan over a low burner or candle warmer. The wine is lighted and poured over the sauce, which in turn can be spooned over the spaghetti while still ablaze.

Many people don't like chicken livers, but they are the main ingredient in several pasta dishes—this dish should change their minds—but it can also be made with raw scallops or shrimp that

80

have been shelled and deveined. Lobster or crab meat can be used; so can tiny meatballs that have been cooked separately, as well as cooked beef or veal or chicken that have been cut into half-inch pieces.

This dish is a fine first course before barbecued steaks or chops, and it makes a fine hot dish for a buffet. As a main course, it might be preceded by antipasto and followed by a green salad. A California Chardonnay for the wine, lemon sherbet, and *caffe corretto*, which is espresso "corrected" with a dash of anisette liqueur, completes the dinner.

THE PASTA

Spaghetti, spaghettini, or linguine.

SET 6 QUARTS WATER TO BOIL, WITH 2 TABLESPOONS SALT; THIS MAY TAKE HALF AN HOUR.

1 POUND SPAGHETTI

PUT SPAGHETTI IN THE BOILING WATER AND COOK 8–9 MINUTES, OR UNTIL DONE, BUT STILL FIRM.

3 tablespoons butter
1 medium onion, finely chopped
1 garlic clove, minced
2 slices bacon or ham, chopped
½ pound mushrooms, sliced
½ teaspoon salt
¼ teaspoon freshly ground
    black pepper
½ pound chicken livers,
    coarsely chopped

In a large skillet or chafing dish, over medium heat, melt the butter and cook the onions, garlic, and bacon until the onions are soft. Add the mushrooms and seasonings and cook for 2 minutes, stirring so that the mushrooms are thoroughly coated. Add the chicken livers and stir until they have lost their color, 2–3 minutes.

¼ cup sweet vermouth, Marsala,
    or brandy, warmed

Warm the vermouth, Marsala, or brandy in saucepan over a low burner or other warmer.

81

Drain spaghetti and pour into warm bowl. Light the wine by tipping so that the burner flame ignites the fumes of the wine; or touch a long match to the wine. Pour wine over the sauce.

While the sauce is still flaming, stir it a couple of times, and as it begins to flicker out, pour it over the spaghetti.

¼ cup chopped parsley or chives

Sprinkle with parsley or chives, toss gently, and serve at once.

1 cup freshly grated Parmesan cheese

Serve freshly grated Parmesan on the side.

VARIATIONS

—Use 1 pound raw sea scallops, cut up, or 1 pound raw, shelled and deveined shrimp.

—Use a meatball recipe (see page 105), making the meatballs tiny and cooking them ahead.

—Use 2 cups cooked beef, veal, or chicken cut into half-inch pieces.

NOTE

Spaghetti alla Fegatini di Pollo varies in taste, depending on what wine is used for flaming. All fortified wines, including sherries and ports, will flame, but not so readily as brandy; a spoonful of brandy may be added to the warmed wine to insure a good blaze. Though the flaming isn't at all necessary to the success of this dish, it mutes the taste of the wine, which should not be as noticeable as the taste of the chicken livers.

Spaghetti alla Marinara
Spaghetti with Sailor's Sauce

for 4–6   10 MINUTES

When the Neapolitan wants to change from Aglio e Olio, he adds some tomatoes and calls it marinara. This changes everything, and calls for the addition of practically anything. In the spring, this sauce is made with fresh tomatoes and fresh basil and called Primavera, particularly in Roman restaurants. In Naples, it's just as apt to be called Salsa di Pomodoro alla Napolitana (Pomorola for short), especially if you start out by sautéeing a sliced onion and chopped carrot in the hot oil. It is supposed to be a light sauce.

Why a tomato sauce should be named after sailors is a mystery, except that sailors brought back tomatoes from the New World to revolutionize Italian cooking, glorifying it or ruining it, depending on whom you talk to. Certainly, tomatoes came to dominate many Italian dishes in the nineteenth century, and indeed, tomatoes have an affinity for oil, garlic, and pungent herbs like oregano and basil, not to mention pasta.

We present a basic Marinara recipe here, quite enough to serve four to six people, except that guests are greedy for this sauce. A longer-cooking variation that makes more sauce is Friday Sauce (see page 110). There are also many variations presented, because it can be varied so easily, or used in so many pasta dishes that go in the oven. It is the simplest and best of tomato sauces that can be prepared quickly.

83

PASTA PRONTO!

Spaghetti alla Marinara is an excellent first course when one hungers for the taste of tomatoes. It can be followed by main courses that are bland, like sautés of chicken, veal, or fish, and various grilled meats. A salad and a light dessert like fruit or berries with Marsala might complete the meal.

Tomatoes are not good companions for delicate wine; the tart acidity of them masks any subtleties of a fine vintage. Rough, coarse, young wines are wanted, something like an ordinary Chianti or Valpolicella, or a regional red from the Spanish Rioja, the French Rhone, or a jug wine of California like a Mountain Red, Barbera, or Zinfandel. With such wines, the tartness of the Sailor's Sauce doesn't matter.

THE PASTA

Spaghetti or spaghettini is generally preferred, although oval linguine, vermicelli, and fine noodles are often used, including those called maccheroni and lingue de passeri.

SET 6 QUARTS WATER TO BOIL, WITH 2 TABLESPOONS SALT; THIS MAY TAKE HALF AN HOUR.

½ cup olive oil
3 cloves garlic, chopped
4 cups canned Italian plum tomatoes, drained and chopped, or 2 pounds fresh tomatoes, peeled, seeded and chopped
½ teaspoon salt
¼ teaspoon freshly ground black pepper
½ cup finely chopped fresh parsley

Heat oil in a skillet or saucepan, add the garlic and cook until the bits are soft, or less than a minute. Add the tomatoes, salt, pepper, and half the parsley. Cook 2–3 minutes, or until hot, but still retaining the tomatoes' shape. (See Note.) Add oregano at the last minute.

84

1 teaspoon fresh oregano
   or ½ teaspoon dried

1 POUND SPAGHETTI	PUT SPAGHETTI IN THE BOILING WATER AND COOK 7–8 MINUTES, OR UNTIL DONE, BUT STILL FIRM.
1 tablespoon butter (optional) 1 cup freshly grated Parmesan cheese	Drain spaghetti and dump into a hot bowl. The butter may be added to the sauce at the last minute to smooth it, or to coat the spaghetti. Add 2 cups of the sauce and toss gently. Sprinkle remaining parsley over the tossed spaghetti. Serve the rest of the sauce on the side, along with a bowl of the freshly grated cheese.

VARIATIONS

—6–12 fresh basil leaves, coarsely chopped, can be added or substituted for the oregano.

—Thyme or marjoram, or both, can be substituted for the oregano.

—At the beginning of the recipe, sauté 4 slices of bacon (or as much as ¼ pound) in the skillet until just beginning to brown. Pour off all but 2 tablespoons of fat, then add ¼ cup of olive oil and proceed.

—Add 3–4 anchovies, cut up, with the tomatoes. Omit the salt.

—Skin 1 pound of Italian sausages, sweet, hot, or both. Crumble the sausage meat into ¼ cup of dry red or white wine, or dry or sweet vermouth. Cook until the wine has evaporated and the sausage is lightly browned. Pour off the fat and add to the sauce.

—Add as much as a pound of shelled and deveined raw shrimp, lobster, or cut-up fish fillets to the sauce, and cook 5–8

85

minutes longer. A tablespoon of fresh tarragon, or a teaspoon of dried, adds to the flavor.

—Sauté a cut-up strip of bacon with a large chopped onion until the onion is transparent. Crumble in 1 pound of lean ground round or chuck, stirring until the meat has lost its color and has begun to brown. Add to the sauce as soon as the tomatoes have begun to cook.

—Soak 2–3 dried Italian mushrooms (or half-ounce package) in warm water for 5 minutes, drain, chop, and add with the tomatoes.

NOTE

Both fresh tomatoes and drained canned tomatoes vary in taste and texture and looks, depending on how long they cook. The recipe given here calls for cooking the tomatoes for 2–3 minutes, which produces a fresh-tasting and lumpy sauce—delicious. When the tomatoes cook for 5 minutes, they are loose and satiny and pale orange—excellent as a sauce. When the tomatoes cook for nearly 20 minutes, they are thick and velvety and rich in taste—producing an exceptional, smooth sauce. (Tomatoes become watery after about 5 minutes of cooking and remain so until the water evaporates and they have been pretty well reduced, which takes just about 20 minutes.) Further cooking reduces the tomatoes still more and concentrates the flavor.

This is a quick version of Friday Sauce (page 110), the simplest of long-cooked sauces.

Spaghetti alla Puttanesca

for 4–6   20 MINUTES

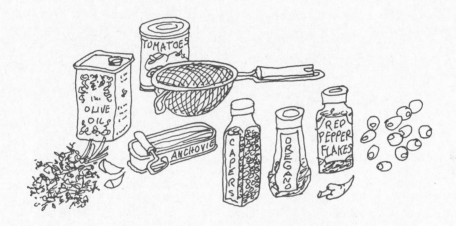

The tomato sauce of Naples called Marinara has a version called *puttanesca,* or *meretrice,* which mean harlot. The sauce consists of off-the-shelf items like capers, olives, and anchovies added quickly to the tomatoes and garlicky oil to make something hot and spicy. An elegant touch is to discard the garlic after it has seasoned the oil, leaving behind only a suspicion.

This recipe is included, not only for its goodness, but because it shows how a basic sauce can be varied, even transformed. Changes in a sauce may be subtle, or frank as Puttanesca. It is a

87

meal in itself when followed by green salad and fruit. Small amounts can be served as a first course, followed by a hearty salad and a liqueur like Strega for dessert. Shrimp with Green Sauce might precede it (page 170). Any rough red wine, Chianti or California Barbera, suits the dish fine.

THE PASTA
Any spaghetti, preferably thin, or vermicelli or linguine.

SET 6 QUARTS WATER TO BOIL, WITH 2 TABLESPOONS SALT; THIS MAY TAKE HALF AN HOUR.

3 tablespoons olive oil
2 garlic cloves, chopped
2 cups canned Italian plum tomatoes, sieved, or 3 ripe tomatoes, peeled, seeded, and chopped
1 tablespoon capers, drained
12 pitted black olives, halved
1 small, hot chili pepper, or ¼ teaspoon crushed red pepper flakes
6 anchovy fillets, drained and chopped
1 teaspoon fresh oregano, chopped, or ½ teaspoon dried
2 tablespoons finely chopped fresh parsley
¼ teaspoon freshly ground pepper

Heat oil in a large skillet, add garlic and cook until soft. Remove garlic, add tomatoes, capers, olives, and chili pepper; and cook for 10 minutes, or until sauce is no longer watery.

Add anchovies, oregano, parsley, and pepper. Turn heat down and cook 10 minutes longer. Taste and add salt if necessary. When sauce is done, remove chili pepper, if used, and discard.

1 POUND SPAGHETTI

BEFORE SAUCE HAS FINISHED COOKING, PUT SPAGHETTI IN THE BOILING WATER AND COOK 8–9 MINUTES, OR UNTIL DONE, BUT STILL FIRM.

Drain spaghetti and pour into a hot bowl. Pour sauce over it and toss gently. Serve at once.

VARIATIONS

—If small whole chili pepper has been used, it can be finely chopped, and all or part of it added to the sauce for extra hotness, instead of being discarded.

—The anchovies can be added just before the tomatoes and be allowed to cook down to a paste. Twice as many as called for can be used; the amounts of capers and olives might be doubled, and so can the tomatoes, in which case the initial cooking time may need to be increased.

—All or part of the garlic can be left in. Chop finely or mince if it is to be left in.

Peperonata
Pepper Sauce

for 4–6   15 MINUTES

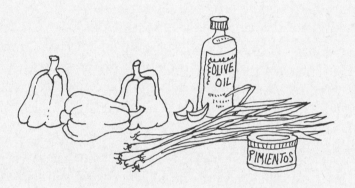

Peppers in one form or another are used almost as freely as tomatoes and garlic in the Italian kitchen, perhaps most appetiz-
ingly in this dish, which is prepared in dozens of ways. Peperonata without pasta is served as a side dish, to grilled and roasted
meats. But this version is excellent with spaghetti, as a first
course, or as accompaniment for cold meats.

Most versions of Peperonata call for slicing the peppers and
cooking them until soft with onions that have been cooked in

90

olive oil and butter or lard, then adding tomatoes. The dish is a treat for the eyes, a crisp mélange that is bright green and red and yellow. Yellow peppers are hard to find—just the others will do.

Italians make a point of peeling peppers. They hold them on a fork above an open burner, turn them slowly, allowing them to char until they blister. They are then held under running water, and the skins are slipped off. This imparts a smoky taste.

Some people like Peperonata without cheese, others insist on clouds of Parmesan. Still others insist on having hot sausages with the dish, but not in it. In any case, plenty of red wine is called for, preferably a light Chianti, Nebbiolo, or California Barbera. As a main course, Peperonata might be preceded by antipasto, followed by a green salad containing mushrooms and cauliflower, raw or cooked, and a dessert like Zabaglione (page 184) or cold melon with Marsala poured in the hollows. Espresso and grappa would make a fine conclusion.

THE PASTA
Spaghetti, thick or thin.

SET 6 QUARTS WATER TO BOIL, WITH 2 TABLESPOONS SALT; THIS MAY TAKE HALF AN HOUR.

2 tablespoons butter
¼ cup olive oil
3 garlic cloves, minced
3 large peppers, green, yellow, and red (if possible, otherwise green and red or all green), peeled (if you want), seeded, chopped

Heat the butter and olive oil in a large skillet over moderate heat. Add the garlic, peppers, onions, and seasonings.

PASTA PRONTO!

6 scallions (green onions),
    white part only, chopped;
    but set aside tops
½ teaspoon salt
¼ teaspoon freshly ground
    pepper
½ teaspoon oregano

Cook for 5 minutes, reduce heat, cover and cook for 10 minutes. (Add some water or dry white wine if the sauce gets too dry.)

1 POUND SPAGHETTI

BEFORE SAUCE HAS FINISHED COOKING, PUT SPAGHETTI IN THE BOILING WATER AND COOK 8–9 MINUTES, OR UNTIL DONE, BUT STILL FIRM.

tops of the scallions, chopped
2 pimientos, chopped

Drain spaghetti and pour into a warm bowl. Add the pepper mixture, toss gently, sprinkle with the green onion tops and the pimientos.

VARIATIONS

—Squeeze the juice of half a lemon over the peppers just before they are taken off the heat.

—Peperonata generally calls for tomatoes, especially when served as a pasta side dish. Use a can (2 pounds, 3 ounces) of Italian plum tomatoes or 4 good-sized fresh ones. The canned tomatoes should be drained, and seeded by forcing them through a sieve or food mill; the fresh ones can be peeled, seeded, and chopped. Tomatoes are added after the pepper mixture has cooked 5 minutes.

Spaghettini con Piselli
Pasta with Peas

for 4–6   10 MINUTES

Fresh peas are a glory of the Italian spring; no country dotes on them more. Peas find their way into a variety of dishes, particularly thin pasta. All sorts of fresh vegetables do so in their seasons—asparagus to zucchini. The vegetable is cooked separately, then added with a basic sauce to the pasta. Zucchini and eggplant are sizzled to browness in oil, cauliflower and broccoli are boiled in salted water and then turned in butter. Peas may have to be parboiled before being added to the sauce, and provide the best sauce of all.

The basic sauce is made by chopping in succession, on a board, a garlic clove or two, an onion, parsley or some other leafy herb, maybe a stalk of celery, a carrot, a green pepper—so that the flavors mingle. Tomatoes are often added, or mushrooms. This is the *battuto*. A dice of salt port, bacon, or ham may be included, or first rendered in a skillet. When the *battuto*

93

is cooked in the salt pork or in olive oil and/or butter, it becomes the *soffrito*—the basic sauce. The method here calls for incorporating partly cooked peas in the sauce, which some people find easier than trying to get the sauce and separately cooked peas to finish at the same time as the pasta.

Fresh vegetables with pasta call for plenty of freshly grated Parmesan or Pecorino Romano, or both, and white wines like Soave or Verdicchio, or Chenin Blanc from California. Peas and pasta make a good first course before grilled fish or a tuna-fish salad. As a main course, it might be preceded by something cold from the sea—oysters or clams or shrimp, with a Green Sauce (page 170)—followed by a salad of endive/or Boston lettuce and sliced oranges. Fruit tarts with black coffee and grappa might end the meal.

THE PASTA
Spaghetti or spaghettini, linguine, tagliatelle, or fettuccine, may be used.

SET 6 QUARTS WATER TO BOIL, WITH 2 TABLESPOONS SALT; THIS MAY TAKE HALF AN HOUR.

¼ cup olive oil
¼ pound prosciutto or other
  ham, chopped
1 medium onion, chopped
1 garlic clove, minced
½ cup finely chopped fresh
  parsley

In a large enamelware skillet, heat the oil and add the ham, onion, garlic, and parsley, cooking until the onions are soft.

1 POUND SPAGHETTINI

PUT SPAGHETTINI IN BOILING WATER AND COOK 7–8 MINUTES, OR UNTIL DONE, BUT STILL FIRM.

94

½ cup chicken broth

1–2 cups fresh or frozen peas,
  parboiled

2 medium tomatoes, peeled,
  seeded, and chopped, or
  1 cup canned Italian plum
  tomatoes, drained and
  chopped

1 tablespoon chopped fresh
  basil or 1 teaspoon dried

½ teaspoon salt

¼ teaspoon freshly ground
  pepper

2 tablespoons butter

1 cup grated Parmesan cheese

Add the broth, and the peas which have been partially cooked but are still quite firm. Cook until the peas are almost done, then add the tomatoes and basil, salt and pepper, and cook for 2–3 minutes longer.

Drain spaghettini and dump into a warm bowl. Add the sauce and butter and half the cheese. Toss gently and serve at once, with remaining cheese on the side.

VARIATIONS

—When canned tomatoes are used, they might well be put in before the peas and cooked for 10 minutes, providing a rich taste rather than a fresh one.

—A simpler version—which can be done in a chafing dish—can be made by sautéeing the ham and ¼ pound sliced mushrooms in 6 tablespoons of butter, adding the cooked peas and then the drained spaghettini, and tossing with some of the cheese. Three eggs, lightly beaten, can be stirred in.

Spaghettini alla Funghi
Spaghettini with Mushrooms

for 4–6   10 MINUTES

When mushrooms are the basic ingredient of any sauce, Italian restraint suggests nothing else should be added, except for a sliced onion, perhaps, to add zest. But Italian gusto urges fresh peas in spring, perhaps some slivers of pepper during the summer, a julienne of ham or chicken in cold weather, or the additions of this particular recipe.

96

Dried mushrooms are often used instead of fresh. These are first soaked in warm water for 5 minutes, particularly when the mushrooms are going to be combined with meats and tomatoes; save the water to thin the sauce later.

Thin pasta, like spaghettini or vermicelli or fettuccine, is particularly suited to most mushroom sauces. Spaghettini alla Funghi makes a fine main course, perhaps preceded by antipasto. As a first course or side dish, it is excellent with grilled steaks, followed by a salad and cheese. Red wines like Barolo, and the California Cabernet Savignon suit such a meal, and the dessert might be Poached Pears with Marsala (page 186).

THE PASTA
Spaghettini or thin noodles, like tagliatelle or linguine.

SET 6 QUARTS WATER TO BOIL, WITH 2 TABLESPOONS SALT; THIS MAY TAKE HALF AN HOUR.

4 slices bacon cut into 1-inch pieces
4 tablespoons butter
½ cup chopped shallots or onions
1 pound fresh mushrooms, sliced, or 2 ounces dried
½ cup dry white wine, dry vermouth, or chicken broth
½ cup finely chopped fresh parsley
¼ teaspoon freshly ground black pepper
¼ teaspoon salt

In a large enamelware skillet, cook the bacon until it just begins to brown, then pour off all but 1 tablespoon of fat. Leave in bacon.

Add the butter; cook shallots or onions until soft; add mushrooms and do the same—in all about 5 minutes.

97

PASTA PRONTO!

1 POUND SPAGHETTINI

PUT SPAGHETTINI IN BOILING WATER AND COOK 7–8 MINUTES, OR UNTIL DONE, BUT STILL FIRM.

Add wine or broth, parsley, and seasonings. Simmer 5 minutes, or until liquid has almost evaporated.

½ cup heavy cream, warmed
½ cup grated Parmesan cheese

Drain spaghettini and turn into warm bowl. Stir warm cream into mushrooms, pour them over the spaghettini, and toss gently. Add cheese and toss again. Serve at once. Serve extra cheese if needed.

VARIATIONS

—Instead of bacon, 4 ounces of prosciutto or other ham, chopped or cut in thin strips, can be lightly browned in 2 tablespoons of butter.

—A cup of cooked peas may be added at the end, during the final simmering. Other cooked vegetables to add are French-cut string beans, diced zucchini, or diced eggplant; in such cases, use only ½ pound mushrooms.

—Any creamed vegetable, or creamed chicken or seafood, may be added in place of the cream.

—Omit cream and squeeze the juice of half a lemon over the mushrooms before they are poured over the spaghettini.

PASTA NON PRONTO

Pasta non Pronto

Many Italian sauces—splendid essences—cook for hours. They are an entire and separate category, stemming from the days when great pots were kept simmering on the back of wood-burning stoves, when game and wildfowl were plentiful.

A collection of quick pasta dishes scarcely includes recipes for long-cooked sauces, except that they can be made ahead, refrigerated, and quickly warmed up—thus greatly extending the range of dishes that can be made at the last minute.

A stock of long-cooking sauces on hand makes the preparation of any pasta pronto dish easy, as well as casseroles and oven dishes like lasagne or manicotti (pages 114 and 130). Many Italian dishes can be varied by simply changing the sauce. Friday sauce (page 110) or Meat-and-Tomato Sauce (page 102) makes a hearty lasagne, for instance, while Ragú Bolognese (page 108) makes a richer one. One or another can be used to vary an omelet or to heighten the flavor of scrambled eggs. They can be used to sharpen the taste of a soup or stew. Mixed with equal parts of wine, water, or stock, they can become a simmering liquid for browned chops or tough cuts of meat like flank steak.

Long-cooked sauces are a comfort to have on hand. Many cooks make double batches of the recipes given here, so that there will be some left over for freezing. Cooled and then put in pint-sized containers, they take up little space in your freezer. They can be thawed quickly in a saucepan over low heat, some water or wine being added to speed the process.

Meat-and-Tomato Sauce

for 6–8   1½ HOURS

Once a cook has found a spaghetti sauce he likes or has developed to suit his special taste, he is apt to brook no changes or consider no alternative, and discountenance all others as without merit. For those not yet committed to their own sauce or who seek a change, a good area of exploration is somebody else's sworn-by recipe. Then, with knowledge of the ways in which variations can be played, the cook can improve his own versions.

The most basic Meat-and-Tomato Sauce starts with ground meat and onions cooked in oil until the meat has lost its red color and the onions are limp; with 4 pounds of canned tomatoes added, salt and pepper, and cooking for an hour's time, a very good sauce results. It is a Marinara Sauce with meat.

The tomatoes can be enriched with canned tomato paste, purée, or sauce. The sauce can be thinned with water, wine, or stock—or combinations of these. Garlic can be incorporated. Seasonings can be basil, oregano, bay leaf, or thyme—or all four. Chopped parsley is good any time, cooked in or strewn on top of servings. Sugar, which seems an unlikely ingredient, is considered essential by many cooks, particularly Italian ones, who like to counteract the acidity of the tomatoes. Hotness, supplied by red pepper flakes or Tabasco sauce, is a matter of taste that can be a pleasing accent or a hot touch.

This recipe, which boasts practically all of the optional additions, was arrived at by a young housewife who uses spaghetti to stretch the budget. She makes the sauce in vast quantities, freezing it in one-pint containers for various uses later.

For a meal of pasta with Meat and Tomato Sauce, Oranges and Olives (page 176) is a good first course, to be eaten while sipping drinks, perhaps vermouth on-the-rocks. A leafy salad and crusty bread go well with the pasta, and the best dessert may be something crunchy, like anise cookies or macaroons, to accompany a lemon sherbet. Espresso and chilled anisette or any of the various licorice-flavored liqueurs might follow.

THE PASTA
Any kind at all.

1 tablespoon olive oil	In a heavy skillet, heat the oil and
1 pound ground beef	crumble the ground beef into it. Brown
1 medium yellow onion,	the meat lightly, break it up and separate
chopped	the pieces. Add the onion as the meat

1 2–pound 3–ounce can Italian
   tomatoes, drained
4 8–ounce cans tomato sauce
1 6–ounce can tomato paste

½ teaspoon freshly ground
   pepper
1½ teaspoons salt
2½ teaspoons oregano
½ teaspoon thyme
¼ teaspoon crushed red
   pepper flakes
1 bay leaf
2 cloves garlic, minced

1 teaspoon sugar
1 tablespoon olive oil

cooks. When the meat is brown and the onion transparent, pour off the fat and transfer the contents of the skillet to a 3–quart saucepan, preferably an enameled one. (Iron pots are not good to cook tomatoes in, because they impart an unpleasant taste).

With the saucepan over low heat, add the tomato products and bring to a simmer.

Add the rest of the ingredients, except for the sugar and olive oil. Cook, uncovered, over low heat for 1½ hours, stirring occasionally. Add a small amount of hot water if the sauce gets too dry during cooking. Skim off any fat from the surface, this will be a residue from the ground beef. Check seasoning.

Half an hour before sauce is done, stir in the sugar and olive oil. This much oil is not enough to make the sauce greasy, but, with the sugar, it rounds out the taste.

Spaghetti con Polpette
Spaghetti with Meatballs

for 6–8   ABOUT 1 HOUR

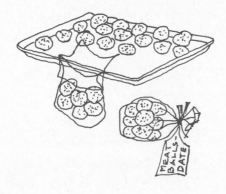

This familiar dish has practically become American by adoption, a standby for family meals and informal parties. It is given here with its own tomato sauce, but any good, ready-made and meatless tomato sauce could be used and the meatballs added—6–8 cups for the quantity of meatballs given. The whole recipe can be frozen. The meatballs alone can be frozen before browning; put them on a cookie sheet to freeze, and then seal groups of them in plastic bags.

105

The polpette (meatballs) are called *polpettine* when they are the size of marbles, and some people prefer them that way. The tiny balls are cooked by the time they are browned, and do not require simmering in the sauce.

Spaghetti and meatballs are usually served as a main course, preceded or followed by almost anything, but a salad of cooked string beans (page 176) seems to suit it particularly. Fruit may be the best dessert. Any red wine—Barolo, Chianti, California Italian types—tastes good.

THE PASTA
Spaghetti, thick or thin; macaroni, large or small; noodles, any size or shape.

SAUCE

2 tablespoons olive oil
1 medium onion, finely
  chopped
2 garlic cloves, minced
2 2–pound 3–ounce cans Italian plum tomatoes, sieved
2 teaspoons salt
½ teaspoon freshly ground
  pepper
2 teaspoons oregano or basil
  (or 1 teaspoon of each)
1 bay leaf

In a heavy, lidded saucepan, preferably enameled ironware, heat the oil; and slowly cook the onions and garlic until soft, but not brown. Force the tomatoes through a sieve or food mill and add, with the seasonings. Bring to a boil, turn down heat, and simmer, uncovered, for 30 minutes.

Crumble the meat into a large mixing bowl. Add the crumbs and parsley.

MEATBALLS

1½ pounds ground beef
1 slice bread, torn into fine
  crumbs
¼ cup finely chopped fresh
  parsley

Mix the seasonings with the egg and milk, and mix thoroughly with the meat, crumbs, and parsley. Shape into 30 balls about 1 inch in diameter, or 24 larger ones.

106

1½ teaspoons salt
½ teaspoon freshly ground
   pepper
½ teaspoon basil
½ teaspoon marjoram
½ teaspoon grated lemon rind
1 egg, beaten
¼ cup milk

2 tablespoons olive oil
2 tablespoons butter

In a heavy skillet, heat the oil and butter. When the foam subsides, put in the meatballs, a few at a time, shaking the pan and turning the balls to brown on all sides. Remove with a slotted spoon to the simmering sauce. Cover and cook ½ hour, on a very low heat. Skim off fat, check sauce seasoning.

VARIATIONS

—Substitute a couple of leaves of fresh sage, finely chopped, for the parsley.

—Add a caper or two to each meatball.

—Add as much as 2 tablespoons of pine nuts and two of raisins to the meatball mixture.

—Add 6–8 chopped olives to the mixture, either green or black.

—Ground pork or veal may be substituted for part of the ground beef; or some ground ham or dried beef may be added.

—One-fourth cup of grated Parmesan or other grated cheese may be added to the meat mixture.

Ragú Bolognese
Bolognese Meat Sauce

for 4–6   ABOUT 1½ HOURS

This famous sauce from the north of Italy is a change from the usual Meat-and-Tomato Sauce (page 102) we are all familiar with. It has chopped vegetables and chicken livers in it, as well as ground meat, and is finished with heavy cream. It can be used as a sauce on any kind of pasta, or as a substitute for the meat-and-tomato sauce called for in Lasagne (page 114) and other casseroles. Use very lean meat to avoid an excess of fat other than the bacon fat and butter that are intrinsic to the dish. The sauce can be skimmed to remove fat before adding the cream at the end.

Ragú Bolognese is so rich that it should be preceded by something light, like melon with prosciutto, followed by a green salad, then fresh strawberries for dessert. If you use the dish as a first course, serve small portions—perhaps before barbecued chicken.

The best wines are none too good for this classic dish—a Barolo or Chianti in a regular bottle (not straw-covered), a Volnay

108

or Beaune from Burgundy, a Cabernet Sauvignon or Pinot Noir from California. Extra dry champagne or Asti Spumante might be served with the strawberries.

THE PASTA
Fine noodles, like fettuccine or tagliatelle.

4 strips lean bacon, finely chopped
1 small onion, finely chopped
1 medium carrot, finely chopped
2 stalks celery, finely chopped
1 pound ground lean beef

½ cup dry white wine
1 cup canned chicken broth
2 cups canned Italian tomatoes, chopped
1 teaspoon salt
¼ teaspoon pepper
2 whole cloves

¼ pound chicken livers, chopped
½–1 cup heavy cream, warmed
grating or sprinkling of nutmeg

In a heavy, lidded 10–12-inch skillet, preferably enameled ironware, cook the bacon in the butter until it is just golden. Add the chopped onion, carrot, and celery, and cook slowly over low heat, stirring, until the vegetables are just tender. Crumble in the ground beef, and cook, stirring and breaking up the lumps until they have lost their pink color and begin to brown.

Pour in the wine and cook until almost all the liquid has evaporated. Add the chicken broth, tomatoes, salt, pepper, and cloves. Cover and cook on very low heat for 1 hour, stirring occasionally.

Skim off any fat, add the chicken livers and cook, uncovered, for 5 minutes. Add the cream, enough to make the sauce the consistency you like. Stir in the sprinkle of nutmeg, check seasoning, and let the sauce heat through, but do not boil. If it is to be used later in the day or frozen, omit the cream and add when reheating to serve.

Makes about 4 cups.

Friday Sauce

for 6–8

1 HOUR

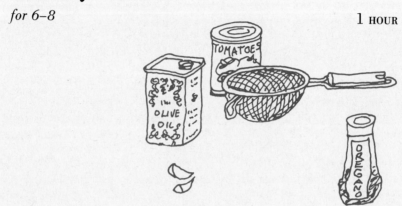

Italian Americans dubbed this meatless tomato sauce Friday Sauce because it was a favorite for those meatless Fridays. It is a basic Marinara Sauce, and like its more quickly cooked version (see Spaghetti alla Marinara, page 83), lends itself beautifully to the addition of seafood. Good any day of the week, Friday Sauce can be varied almost as many ways as the quick Marinara, but is best when used by itself with all its simple richness; it is also good with meatballs.

Squeezing the tomatoes through the hands is a traditional way of breaking up the tomatoes, but for a smoother sauce they can be sieved, that is, forced through a strainer or food mill before cooking. Alternately, the whole sauce can be sieved after cooking.

Any olive oil that appears on the surface of the cooked sauce can be skimmed off if desired, or stirred in as it is served.

The recipe can be frozen.

THE PASTA
Any kind at all.

½ cup olive oil
2 garlic cloves, chopped

2 2-pound, 3-ounce cans
    Italian tomatoes, well
    broken up
2 teaspoons salt
½ teaspoon freshly ground
    pepper
2 teaspoons oregano

Put the olive oil and garlic in a heavy, three-to-four quart saucepan, preferably enamelware, and cook slowly until the garlic is soft, but not brown. Quickly pour in the tomatoes, all at once, before the garlic browns. Poured in too slowly, the tomatoes will splutter and splash.

Add the seasonings, stir, and bring to a boil. Turn down to a simmer, and cook uncovered, on very low heat, for 1 hour, stirring occasionally.

Makes about 6 cups.

VARIATIONS

—Add 6–12 fresh basil leaves, coarsely chopped.

—Add as much as a pound of shelled and deveined raw shrimp about 5 minutes before the end of the cooking. Or add leftover cooked shrimp just long enough to heat through.

—Sauté a cut-up strip of bacon in a skillet with a large chopped onion until the onion is transparent. Crumble in 1 pound of lean ground round or chuck, stirring until the meat has lost its color and begun to brown. Drain meat of all its fat and put in the saucepan when the tomatoes go in.

PASTA AL FORNO

Pasta al Forno

Many pasta dishes can be prepared ahead, then quickly baked in the oven *(al fornô)*. Some of them can be frozen, in all or in part. All that is called for is a supply of sauce already made, fillings that can also be made ahead or made quickly at the last minute, and cooked pasta. What appears to be an elaborate dish is simple to do when preparation and assembly are unhurried. Some of the most popular Italian dishes are made by layering or stuffing cooked pasta and combining them with sauces and cheeses—Cannelloni and Manicotti (page 130), Lasagne (page 114)—heated to bubbling in a hot oven. Baking time is rarely more than half an hour.

All these dishes are filling and are excellent main courses, perhaps best of all with some simple salad, with antipasto before and a light dessert to follow.

Because recipes for pasta al forno look difficult, people rarely cook them at home. But actually, the recipes spell out steps that are simple and particularly easy to vary—by changing the sauce or the cheese. Every version has its own special taste and appearance. When made at home, pasta al forno dishes are invariably better than what is offered in most restaurants. All of them are inexpensive, popular, and make excellent party dishes.

Lasagne

for 6

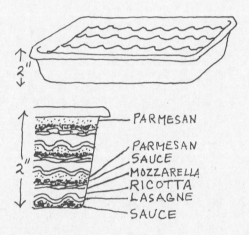

Lasagne is such a hearty main course that it calls for little more than a leafy salad and good crusty bread to go with it. Crisp vegetables and bread sticks with a hot dip like Bagna Cauda (page 171) make a good first course with drinks. The wine should be red and even rough, a Chianti in the straw-covered bottle, a Côte-du-Rhône from France, a Mountain Red from California. Fresh fruit or berries are the simplest of desserts, with espresso and grappa or Italian brandy.

When you check the seasoning of the Lasagne, remember that the cheeses are invariably bland, except for the Parmesan, so don't be hesitant about having plenty of flavor in the sauce. If in

114

doubt, set out a saucer of red pepper flakes so that people can perk thinks up still more. Moistness is important to good Lasagne; do not let the sauce dry out. Put the dish in the oven as late as possible, for it should be eaten as soon as it comes out.

THE PASTA
Curly-edged lasagne noodles, regular or green.

SAUCE

2 tablespoons olive oil
1 pound ground round steak
1 medium onion, chopped
2 garlic cloves, minced
salt and pepper
3½ cups canned Italian
   tomatoes
     (a 1–pound 12–ounce can)
1 6–ounce can tomato paste
1 teaspoon salt
¼ teaspoon freshly ground
   pepper
⅛ teaspoon cayenne pepper
½ teaspoon basil
½ teaspoon oregano
1 bay leaf
½ cup dry red wine
1 cup water

FILLING

1 pound ricotta or creamed
   cottage cheese
8 ounces mozzarella cheese,
   thinly sliced
½ cup grated Parmesan cheese

SET 6 QUARTS WATER TO BOIL; THIS MAY TAKE HALF AN HOUR.

In a large, heavy skillet, preferably enameled ironware, heat the oil, and crumble in the ground meat. Cook, stirring and breaking up the lumps with a fork or wooden spoon, until the pink is gone and the meat is lightly browned. As the meat cooks, add the onion and garlic. Pour off any fat, and sprinkle with salt and pepper.

Add the tomatoes, tomato paste, seasonings, wine, and water. (The wine can be omitted and the water increased to 1½ cups.) Simmer 1½ hours, uncovered, stirring occasionally. If the sauce gets too thick, add hot water in small amounts. Skim off fat and check seasoning. Remove bay leaf.

115

PASTA

8 OUNCES LASAGNE NOODLES
1 tablespoon olive oil

ADD 2 TABLESPOONS SALT TO 6 QUARTS BOILING WATER. ADD THE NOODLES AND THE OIL, AND COOK 10–12 MINUTES, OR UNTIL THE NOODLES ARE DONE, BUT STILL A LITTLE FIRM. STIR OCCASIONALLY WITH A WOODEN FORK TO KEEP THEM SEPARATED. DRAIN AND PUT BACK IN THE POT.

In a baking dish long enough to hold the noodles, wide enough for 3 noodles in a row, and about 2 inches deep, spread a thin layer of the tomato and meat mixture (the sauce) in the bottom of the dish. Divide the noodles, the rest of the sauce and the cheeses (the filling) into 3 more or less equal parts. Starting with the noodles, make 3 layers of ingredients in this order: noodles, ricotta, mozzarella, sauce, Parmesan cheese. Bake, covered with foil, in preheated, 350° oven for 20 minutes. Uncover and bake 5 minutes longer, or until just bubbling.

GARNISH

¼ cup finely chopped fresh
parsley

Sprinkle with parsley.

VARIATIONS

—The Meat-and-Tomato Sauce on page 102 can be used as a substitute for the sauce recipe given here. It takes the same length of time to cook—1½ hours. Freeze any leftover sauce.

—Ragú Bolognese, on page 108, can be substituted for this sauce. Expand with canned tomato sauce or canned chicken or beef broth to make 5 cups. Or double the Ragú Bolognese recipe as

116

given, and then freeze any leftover sauce. In either case, omit the cream. This sauce takes 1 hour to cook.

—The sauce in the Noodle Casserole recipe (page 118) can be used. Add canned tomato sauce to make 4–5 cups. Check seasoning; it might need perking up with some red pepper flakes or herbs. This sauce takes only the time necessary to brown the ground meat.

—Also, the filling in the Noodle Casserole recipe (page 118) can be used. Add another ½ cup sour cream and 8 ounces shredded mozzarella cheese to Noodle Casserole Filling for a delicious Lasagne filling.

—The bacon and ground meat variation for Marinara Sauce, page 83, can be used as sauce for Lasagne with added canned or fresh tomatoes that have been cooked 2–3 minutes. Check seasoning. This sauce takes only the 2–3 minutes the tomatoes cook, plus the time the ground meat takes to brown.

—Substitute the sausage variation of the Marinara Sauce (page 83) with added canned or fresh tomatoes that have been cooked 2–3 minutes. Check seasoning. This sauce takes about the same time as the preceding one.

NOTE

The Lasagne sauce is good used as a meat-and-tomato sauce for any pasta. It can be stretched, if necessary, by the addition of canned tomato sauce, canned beef broth, or even water if it is very thick and rich. Check and adjust seasonings after additions.

Noodle Casserole

for 6   20–30 MINUTES TO BAKE

PARSLEY
SAUCE
NOODLES
FILLING
NOODLES

Americans love casseroles, and there's scarcely a family in the land that doesn't have a favorite or two. Here is one of ours, with a fresh taste and lightness that is unexpected and satisfying, to be served with a big green salad and crusty bread. A white wine like Soave or a California Chenin Blanc, a Grenache Rosé, or a light red like Bardolino will all taste good with the casserole. The white wines would go best with a first course of antipasto. For those who prefer to serve the salad as a separate course, the noodle dish might be accompanied by broccoli or green beans. Dessert might well be strawberries or blueberries or raspberries, left for 5 minutes or so in a bowl with a few dollops

118

of Marsala, and a sprinkle of sugar, to be followed by grappa or brandy or kirsch and strong black coffee.

THE PASTA

Noodles one-half to three-quarter inches wide are good for this casserole. Cook them until they are *al dente*, or still slightly firm. The time will vary with the width of the noodles, but is usually less than the time indicated on the package.

SAUCE

1 pound ground beef

1 tablespoon oil

2 8-ounce cans tomato sauce

SET 6 QUARTS WATER TO BOIL; THIS MAY TAKE HALF AN HOUR.

In a heavy skillet, heat the oil and crumble the ground beef into it. Brown the meat lightly; break it up and separate the bits as they cook. Pour off the fat and add the tomato sauce. Remove from heat.

FILLING

1 cup cottage cheese

8 ounces cream cheese

½ cup sour cream

4–6 scallions with green tops, chopped

2 tablespoons finely chopped fresh parsley

1 medium green pepper, chopped

½ teaspoon salt

¼ teaspoon freshly ground pepper

In a mixing bowl, combine the cheeses and sour cream. Mix in the vegetables and salt and pepper.

PASTA

8 OUNCES NOODLES

2 tablespoons salt

1 tablespoon butter

ADD 2 TABLESPOONS SALT AND NOODLES TO 6 QUARTS BOILING WATER. COOK THE NOODLES UNTIL JUST TENDER—ABOUT 5 MINUTES. DRAIN AND RETURN TO THE POT. STIR IN THE BUTTER TO KEEP THE NOODLES FROM STICKING TOGETHER.

119

In a two to two-and-a-half quart casserole or baking dish, spread one half of the noodles. Cover with the cheese mixture (the filling), then cover with the remaining noodles. Spread the meat mixture (the sauce) over the top.

GARNISH

¼ cup finely chopped fresh
   parsley

Bake, uncovered, in a 350° oven for 20–30 minutes.

Sprinkle with parsley.

NOTE

For later serving, cool thoroughly before refrigerating or freezing. To reheat after refrigeration, bring to room temperature, place in preheated, 350° oven, lightly covered with foil, for about 30 minutes. To freeze, carefully remove from casserole or baking dish to heavy foil. Seal and freeze. To reheat, remove from foil and put into an ovenproof dish with a small amount of water, just enough to wet the bottom of the dish. Cover loosely with foil and place in preheated, 350° oven for 45–60 minutes.

Shell Noodles with
Chili con Carne

for 6–8   2½ HOURS

This is a rich and substantial chili, made with chunks of beef instead of ground beef. The noodles take the place of the more customary red beans, to produce a somewhat lighter dish. Italians dote on beans as much as they do on pasta, more or less freely interchanging them, preferring pasta when there is not much time for cooking.

This dish is a main course in itself, good party or family fare, needing no more than a good salad and crusty bread as accompaniment. The salad can be a simple one of shredded lettuce, chopped fresh tomatoes, and green onions; or a fancy one with avocado, thinly sliced red onions, and black olives.

As with bean versions of chili, place a bowl of grated Cheddar cheese on the side, for sprinkling over all. No first course seems called for, unless it might be antipasto. Beer is good to drink with the chili, but a flowery white wine, like Soave or a Chardonnay from California, is often preferred.

Like all pasta casseroles, the chili may need some extra liquid when it is reheated. Start the reheating with a cover on the dish; if liquid is needed, add a little hot water.

121

Chocolate in any form is delicious after chili, perhaps the simplest being ice cream, or a custard over which dark chocolate has been shaved; this is much too rich for sensible people, but much too good to be passed up. Coffee and Cognac are a fine ending.

THE PASTA

Small or medium shell noodles, or little corkscrew ones, or little bows, or small elbow macaroni. Regular noodles could be used, with the Chili con Carne served over them rather than being mixed in.

CHILI CON CARNE

2 pounds beef chuck, or top or bottom round, in ½–¾ inch cubes

3 tablespoons cooking oil

1 medium onion, chopped

1 medium green pepper, chopped

1 tablespoon paprika

1 tablespoon flour

1 16-ounce can tomato purée

hot water if needed

2 cloves garlic, chopped

1 tablespoon salt

¼ teaspoon black pepper

½ teaspoon crushed red pepper flakes

1 teaspoon oregano

½ teaspoon ground cumin

2 tablespoons chili powder, or more

Dry the meat on paper towels for browning, it won't brown if it is wet. Heat the oil in a heavy skillet. When it is hot, add the meat, a few pieces at a time to avoid crowding the pan. As the pieces are browned, remove them, with a slotted spoon, to a heavy, lidded, flameproof casserole.

In the skillet, slowly cook the onions and green pepper until they are soft, but not brown, adding a little more oil if the pan gets dry. Sprinkle in the paprika and flour, stirring until the flour no longer shows white. Add to the meat in the casserole.

Add the tomato puree.

Mash the garlic and salt together, and add with the rest of the seasonings to the casserole. Stir and bring to a simmer. Cover and place in the preheated, 325°

oven. Adjust heat just to maintain the simmer, and cook 1½ to 2 hours, until beef is tender. Stir occasionally, and add hot water in small quantities if liquid gets too thick. Tip pot and skim off fat. Check seasoning and ,add more chili if desired. For more hotness, add more red pepper flakes or a few drops of Tabasco.

PASTA
3 CUPS SHELL NOODLES

COOK NOODLES IN 6 QUARTS BOILING WATER, WITH 2 TABLESPOONS SALT, UNTIL DONE, BUT STILL A LITTLE FIRM.

Drain noodles and stir into the chili, or into a warm bowl if you intend to serve separately. Put chili with noodles back in the oven for 10–15 minutes or until just warmed through.

GARNISH
2 whole pimientos, in strips
¼ cup finely chopped fresh
   parsley

Garnish with pimiento and parsley.

Can be frozen.

Shell Noodles with Curried Shrimp

for 4–6   40 MINUTES

The little shell noodles are both decorative and appropriate in this handsome dish. They complement both the sauce and the shrimp. A bright green vegetable would be a good accompaniment, or at the height of the tomato season, a salad of plain sliced tomatoes with fresh basil (page 178) would be perfect. Dessert might be Biscuit Tortoni (page 183). A white wine like Soave or Frascati, or California Chenin Blanc or Folle Blanche, would taste delicious.

THE PASTA
Small shell noodles, or small bows.

SHRIMP
3 quarts water
1 tablespoon salt
1 celery stalk
2 sprigs parsley
1 bay leaf
1 teaspoon thyme
¼ teaspoon pepper
½ teaspoon saffron threads, crumbled
2 pounds shelled and deveined raw shrimp, fresh or frozen

Put the water in a large saucepan. Add the salt, celery, parsley, bay leaf, thyme, pepper, and saffron, and simmer 20–30 minutes. Bring to a vigorous boil, and put in the shrimp. They are done as soon as they are opaque and take on color—fresh ones, by the time the water comes back to a boil; frozen ones, even before. Drain in a colander, pick out and discard the bay leaf, celery, and parsley. Do not rinse. Spread out on a platter so they won't cook further in their own heat.

124

SET 3 QUARTS OF WATER TO BOIL, WITH
1 TABLESPOON SALT; THIS MAY TAKE 20
MINUTES.

SAUCE

1 tablespoon oil
2 tablespoons butter
1 medium onion, grated
1 garlic clove, minced
1 medium tart apple, peeled,
  cored, and finely chopped
2 tablespoons curry powder
1 teaspoon turmeric
1 teaspoon grated fresh ginger
  or ½ teaspoon ground
½ teaspoon crushed red pepper
  flakes
2 teaspoons flour

1½ cups canned chicken broth
½ teaspoon salt
¼ teaspoon white pepper
2 tablespoons Amontillado or
  cream sherry

Heat the oil and butter in a saucepan.
Add the onion and garlic and cook, stirring, over very low heat until it dries a
bit, but not long enough to stick. Add
the apple and cook until the apple is soft,
mashing it with a fork as it cooks. Stir in
the curry powder, turmeric, ginger, red
pepper flakes, and flour. Remove from
the heat and add the chicken broth, a
little at a time, stirring to mix well. Put
back on the heat, add salt and pepper,
and bring to a simmer, stirring constantly. Cook 2–3 minutes, add sherry.

PASTA AND ASSEMBLY

2 CUPS SMALL SHELL NOODLES
1 cup heavy cream

ADD NOODLES TO THE BOILING WATER.
COOK UNTIL JUST BARELY TENDER, 6–7
MINUTES.

Drain the noodles, put back in the pot.
Add the cooked shrimp, the sauce, and
the cream. Stir gently, and pour into a
baking dish or ovenproof casserole. Cover
lightly with foil and place in preheated,

125

325° oven for 20–30 minutes, until just heated through. It is important not to cook the shrimp further, because they toughen.

GARNISH

½ cup finely chopped fresh parsley

Stir in half the parsley, sprinkle the rest on top.

NOTE

The dish can be assembled before baking, except for the parsley, and refrigerated overnight. If sauce has been absorbed after the dish has been standing, add small amounts of cream or chicken broth, or both before baking.

Macaroni and Cheese

for 4–6   15–20 MINUTES TO BAKE

Macaroni is a versatile standby of the pasta family, easily glorified with a variety of sauces—thin sauces for the small macaroni and thick ones for the larger sizes. Macaroni can be used in place of spaghetti or noodles with the pasta pronto sauces. Macaroni can also be combined with other sauces and cheeses, then finished in the oven to make a casserole. Friday Sauce (page 110) or Meat-and-Tomato Sauce (page 102) might be used, or the

127

creamy sauce given here. With the addition of a cup or so of cooked chicken, shrimp, ham, or tuna fish, it can be a meal in itself.

The recipe presented here—without the additions—is a good accompaniment for grilled or barbecued steaks, chops, hamburgers, and also pan-broiled ham or fish. Antipasto is a good first course. Light red wines like Valpolicella or Bardolino or California Gamay suit the menu, although a white Frascati or Verdicchio might be preferred with fish. A bowl of cherries or strawberries, to be eaten with the fingers, is a pleasant dessert, served with glasses of chilled kirsch or Poire and followed by espresso.

Macaroni and Cheese can be done ahead and refrigerated or frozen, but will need to have extra milk added to restore its creaminess. The milk is added by pouring it down the side rather than over the top.

PASTA

2 CUPS SMALL ELBOW MACARONI
1 tablespoon butter

SAUCE

2 tablespoons butter
1 small onion, finely chopped
½ teaspoon dry mustard
2 tablespoons flour

3 cups milk or light cream, warmed
1 teaspoon salt
¼ teaspoon pepper
1 teaspoon Worcestershire sauce

ADD 1 TABLESPOON SALT AND THE MACARONI TO 3 QUARTS BOILING WATER. COOK ABOUT 5 MINUTES, UNTIL DONE, BUT STILL A LITTLE FIRM. STIR TO KEEP FROM STICKING TO THE BOTTOM. DRAIN AND PUT BACK IN THE POT WITH THE BUTTER, STIRRING TO COAT. THIS IS TO KEEP IT FROM STICKING TOGETHER WHILE IT WAITS FOR THE SAUCE.

In a saucepan, melt 2 tablespoons butter, and slowly cook the onions until they are limp, but not brown. Stir in the mustard and flour.

Remove from the heat and slowly stir in the milk and seasonings. With the pan over low heat, cook, stirring, until the sauce comes to a boil. Simmer 2–3 min-

8 ounces sharp Cheddar cheese,
    grated, about 2 cups
dash of nutmeg

utes. Remove from the heat again, and add the cheese gradually, stirring until it melts. Add the nutmeg. The sauce will be thin. If it should curdle, pour it all into the blender, or beat with a hand or electric beater, blending or beating until smooth.

ASSEMBLY

1 4–ounce can or jar
    pimientos, chopped
1 medium green pepper,
    chopped

Add the sauce to the macaroni, and stir in the pimientos and green pepper. Pour into buttered baking dish or casserole.

¼ cup fine, fresh bread
    crumbs, or herb-seasoned
    crumbs
1 tablespoon butter, melted

Mix the bread crumbs and melted butter, cool and sprinkle over the top. Bake in a preheated, 350° oven for 15–20 minutes, uncovered. This makes a creamy, moist dish. For a drier one, cook 5–10 minutes longer.

GARNISH

2 tablespoons finely chopped
    fresh parsley

Sprinkle with parsley.

Can be frozen.

VARIATIONS

—One of the most delectable additions to Macaroni and Cheese is 18–24 shucked raw oysters, stirred into the macaroni before the crumbs are added. The amount of cheese should be reduced by half; strained juice from the oysters can be substituted for part of the milk in the cream sauce.

—Raw shrimp, shelled and deveined, are a fine addition. Frozen raw shrimp, the kind that are frozen separately, should be dropped into boiling, salted water for about a minute before adding to the macaroni and sauce. The ones frozen in a block should stay in the boiling water just long enough to be separated. Use half as much cheese as in above recipe.

129

Cannelloni and Manicotti
Stuffed Noodle Rolls

for 4–6   15–20 MINUTES TO BAKE

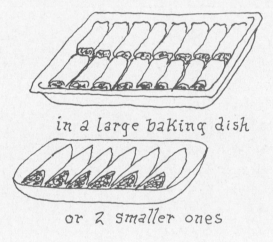

in a large baking dish

or 2 smaller ones

Cannelloni seems to be a modern restaurant invention, at least in Italy, a Roman response to French *quenelles*, those elegant force-meat dumplings bathed in a sauce. Cannelloni are fillings wrapped in squares of cooked, homemade pasta dough, which in turn are covered with sauces and heated to bubbling in the oven. They are not often found on American menus, which is surprising because travelers returning from Italy rave about them. Perhaps it's only a matter of time; but meanwhile, you can easily make Cannelloni at home. And if you don't want to make your

130

own pasta dough, a good substitute is manicotti, the thick ribbed tube of pasta you can buy that is filled and sauced like the cannelloni.

In either case, the cannelloni squares and manicotti tubes are first cooked in boiling water before they are stuffed with filling. This is true of many pasta shapes that are stuffed. Their cousins, ravioli and tortellini, are stuffed first, then boiled in salted water or stock; they are much like Chinese *wontons,* Jewish *kreplach,* and Russian *pelmeny.* Ravioli and tortellini are described here as variations (page 134-135).

Cannelloni and Manicotti are not recommended as first courses because they are too substantial; one is too skimpy a serving and two of them would be overwhelming! As a main course they can be preceded by something cold or something simple—smoked salmon with capers, oysters or clams on the half shell, or a mess of steamed clams or mussels, served with white wine like Frascati or Verdicchio. The pasta itself calls for red wine—a Valpolicella or a California Zinfandel or Gamay. A simple green salad might accompany it, followed by a light dessert of sliced oranges sprinkled with sugar and dribbled with kirsch.

The two fillings presented here can be used to stuff any large packaged pasta—shell noodles, rigatoni, ziti—as well as other homemade pasta shapes—ravioli, tortellini, agnolotti. These are all smaller than cannellonni and manicotti, so more of them will be needed for each serving, perhaps six or eight. Count out a number that would serve four people as a main course, and you will have enough to serve six as a separate course.

The Homemade Dough (page 33) can be made into various shapes and stuffed with either filling—or any other filling you might like to consider. In addition to the cannelloni squares, the little pillows of ravioli and the small twists called tortellini, which are half-rounds with the ends pinched together, can be made with homemade dough. Ravioli and tortellini usually are

131

served as a first course, buttered and sprinkled with cheese, or with tomato sauces, or Il Pesto sauce (page 52) or whatever, depending on the filling.

In the recipe below for Cannelloni and Manicotti, we have distinguished between directions for cooking packaged pasta and homemade dough by putting the latter in italics.

PASTA

12 MANICOTTI TUBES, OR 16
  SQUARES HOMEMADE
  PASTA DOUGH 4 × 4
  INCHES (see page 33).

FILLING

1 10–ounce package frozen
  chopped spinach (or 1
  pound fresh), cooked,
  drained, pressed dry, and
  finely chopped
2 cups ricotta or creamed
  cottage cheese
2 eggs, beaten
2 tablespoons finely chopped
  scallions
salt and freshly ground black
  pepper to taste
good grating of nutmeg

COOKING PACKAGED PASTA

DROP MANICOTTI TUBES CAREFULLY INTO 6 QUARTS BOILING WATER WITH 2 TABLESPOONS SALT. STIR GENTLY AND COOK 6 MINUTES AFTER WATER COMES BACK TO A BOIL. DRAIN, RINSE WITH COLD WATER, AND SET ASIDE ON PAPER TOWELS TO AWAIT STUFFING.

COOKING HOMEMADE PASTA

To make with homemade pasta dough, divide dough into 4 equal parts. Roll each piece into an eight-inch square, and cut into 4 squares. They should be less than one-eighth inch thick. Set on paper towels to dry for an hour. Drop carefully into 6 quarts boiling water with 2 tablespoons salt. Cook for 5 minutes after water comes back to a boil, stirring gently to keep them from sticking together. Drain and set aside on paper towels to await stuffing.

In a mixing bowl, combine the spinach, cheeses, eggs, and scallions. Mix well and add salt, pepper, and nutmeg to taste. Don't make it too bland.

CREAM SAUCE

4 tablespoons butter
4 tablespoons flour
3 cups milk, warmed
¾ teaspoon salt
¼ teaspoon white pepper

In a saucepan, melt the butter and stir in the flour. Take it off the heat, pour in the milk, stirring constantly until sauce is smooth. Put back on the heat and cook, stirring, until it comes to a boil. Add salt and pepper and cook 2–3 minutes, still stirring, until it thickens.

Butter a large shallow baking dish, or 2 smaller ones, that will take the tubes or rolls close together, side by side, in one layer.

Put the filling into the parboiled manicotti tubes, and place them in the baking dish as they are filled.

If homemade pasta dough is used, spread out the squares on wax paper, distribute the filling along the center of each (about 2 good tablespoons), and roll them up. Place, folded side down, in the baking dish, as with the manicotti. (See Note.)

TOPPING

2 cups tomato-meat sauce
  or tomato sauce
¼ cup grated Parmesan cheese

Pour the cream sauce over the tubes or rolls, and let stand for a few minutes to set. Spoon the tomato-meat sauce over all, and sprinkle with Parmesan cheese. (See Note.)

If manicotti has been used, bake uncovered, in preheated, 350° oven for about 20 minutes, until hot, tender, and bubbling.

133

If homemade pasta dough has been used, bake uncovered for about 15 minutes.

GARNISH

¼ cup finely chopped fresh parsley

Sprinkle with parsley and serve immediately.

VARIATIONS

—This meat filling is a wonderful substitute for the spinach-and-cheese filling:

1 tablespoon oil

1 pound lean ground beef

1 10–ounce package frozen chopped spinach (or 1 pound fresh), cooked, drained, pressed dry, and finely chopped

½ cup grated Parmesan cheese

¼ cup fine dry bread crumbs

Heat the oil in a skillet and crumble in the beef. Cook, stirring and breaking up the lumps, until it is lightly brown. Pour off any fat. In a mixing bowl, combine the meat, spinach, Parmesan, and crumbs.

1 garlic clove, chopped

1 teaspoon salt

¼ teaspoon pepper

½ teaspoon oregano

dash of nutmeg

2 eggs, beaten

Mash the garlic with the salt, and add with the other seasonings to the eggs. Combine thoroughly with the meat mixture.

—Here is how you shape homemade pasta dough for ravioli. Use the spinach-and-cheese filling, the meat filling, or any other filling that you wish:

Divide the dough into 8 equal parts and shape into the form of a sausage. Roll out each one paper thin, in strips about 6 inches wide and twice as long. On every other long sheet, place little mounds of your filling (a teaspoonful or less) at one-and-a-half-inch intervals, across and down the strips. Dip the forefinger in water and draw lines on the dough between the mounds and along the edges; this moistening helps the dough to stick together. Place an empty sheet over the filled sheet, pressing down and around the mounds and along the edges to seal. Cut apart into squares with a sharp knife or pastry cutter. Allow to dry for an hour. Cook in batches, in 6 quarts of vigorously boiling water containing 2 tablespoons salt, for 5–9 minutes, or until done. Butter and serve with cheese or sauce. Makes 60 or more ravioli.

—Here are directions for shaping the somewhat difficult tortellini. Fillings are the same as for cannelloni, manicotti, and so forth:

Tortellini are much like ravioli but are formed in a different way. Roll out the dough on a floured board until paper thin. Cut in circles about 3 inches in diameter with a glass or cookie cutter. Place about a teaspoonful of the filling on each circle, wet the edges and fold over, pressing the edges to seal. Curve the straight side around so the points overlap slightly, and press them together. Allow to dry for an hour. Cook and serve the same way as the ravioli. Makes 60 or more tortellini.

NOTE

When a filled pasta is all assembled and ready for the oven, it can be refrigerated for up to 2 days, well covered with foil. Leftovers of these dishes can be frozen.

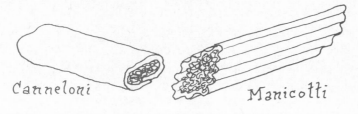

Canneloni   Manicotti

PASTA CON BRIO

Pasta con Brio

Italians are masters at the quick preparation of dishes to accompany a savory pasta—pasta as a first course or as a side dish. In this chapter we present some foods that go especially well with pasta; they are cooked with flair, and are exciting, lively parts of a meal, like the flourishes in music called *con brio*. As for the pasta, you are encouraged to experiment freely with the recipes in the "Pasta Pronto" Chapter.

Some of these dishes, like Veal Marsala (page 143) cook so quickly and simply that they can scarcely be called recipes—which is why they rarely appear in cookbooks or are lost among the complications. We have isolated some of them here. They are among the most delicious of Italian ways with food.

Many other dishes are perfect foils for pasta: stews; pot roasts; roast chicken, veal, and pork. Although these require more attention than Veal Marsala they can be made well ahead of time, and thus, any last minute flurry in the kitchen can be avoided.

Italians tend to serve pasta before stews, but it can also be served with the stew, as with Stufatino alla Romano (page 138). With pot roasts, Italians serve pasta in a special way. The sauce from the pot roast is spooned over the pasta to make the first course before serving the pot roast and a simple vegetable. Thus, a dish like Braciola (page 140) can span two courses.

Roasts of chicken, veal, and pork are usually preceded by pasta. Then the roast is served with something quite simple—maybe only parsley, or sliced tomatoes, or a hot vegetable like string beans. These are attractive ways to vary a meal, older than Rome. In Italy it is done with flair—*con brio*.

137

Stufatino alla Romano
Roman Beef Stew

for 4   1½–2 HOURS

This subtly spicy stew is delicious served with thin noodles like fettucine, with spaghettini, and even with tiny versions of macaroni like capelletti, tossed with butter and Parmesan cheese. Avoid coarser macaronis or large shell noodles because they will mask the flavor of the stew.

No accompanying vegetable is called for—just a cool salad of green beans with an Italian dressing (page 175). A full red wine like Barolo or Chianti or a California Barbera or Zinfandel goes well with the stew and with the antipasto that might precede it. For greater contrast, a first course might be Scallops with Pernod (page 174) and a white wine like Orvieto or a Chenin Blanc from California. A fine dessert would be apples or pears with Bel Paese or Gorgonzola, although some might prefer the fruits stewed or in tarts, served with Strega or Calvados, and plenty of espresso with anise cookies.

THE PASTA

Fettucine, spaghettini, or small macaroni.

138

MEAT

2 pounds beef chuck, or
    boneless shoulder, in
    1-inch cubes
2 tablespoons olive oil,
    more if needed

SEASONINGS

3 cloves garlic, minced
1 teaspoon salt
¼ teaspoon freshly ground
    black pepper
6 cloves, broken up
¼ teaspoon cinnamon
⅛ teaspoon nutmeg
⅛ teaspoon allspice
1 tablespoon chopped fresh
    parsley

ASSEMBLY

½ cup dry red wine
1 1-pound can Italian
    tomatoes, undrained

2 medium green peppers, cut
    into 1-inch squares
2 tablespoons olive oil
12 black olives, pitted
2 tablespoons chopped
    pimientos

Dry the beef on paper towels for browning. In a heavy skillet, heat the oil and brown the meat, a few pieces at a time. As the cubes are done, put them into a lidded, flameproof casserole.

Stir in the garlic and seasonings.

Add the wine, simmer for 1–2 minutes. Add the tomatoes, coarsely chopped, and bring to a simmer. Cover and place in a preheated 325° oven. Turn the oven down to 300°, or whatever temperature will just maintain the simmer. Cook 1½–2 hours, or until the meat is tender. Add hot water in half-cup amounts during cooking if the stew gets too dry. Tip the pot and skim off fat. Check the seasoning.

Heat 2 tablespoons olive oil in a clean skillet and cook the green peppers on a low flame until they are just tender and still bright green. Stir them into the stew, and sprinkle with the olives and pimientos.

Serve with, or on pasta.

Braciola
Beef Roll

for 4   2½ HOURS

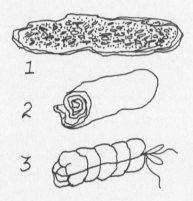

Braciola is a beef roll, browned and cooked in tomato sauce, which not only provides the meat course for a meal and the sauce for the pasta that goes with or goes before, but also makes enough sauce to have with pasta another time.

This flexibility offers all sorts of possibilities for various pot roasts and leftover gravies and sauces. Among them could be considered *braciolini,* which is one of the Italian words for chops, which can also be cooked in sauces; a pocket could be made in thick pork or veal chops, then filled with stuffings, then browned and cooked in a sauce. Small pieces of beef or veal can

140

be flattened, stuffed, and rolled, then browned and stewed in sauce; these are called *uccelletti*, little birds.

If you would like a thicker sauce for this simple beef roll, and less of it, keep the beef warm and cook the sauce over high heat, stirring constantly, until it has reduced to the thickness you seek. Leftover sauce can be frozen.

If you cannot find a piece of round or shoulder beef about a half-inch thick, to be pounded to a quarter inch, get a thicker piece and have the butcher butterfly it. That is, have him slit it horizontally almost all the way through, so that it will open out flat, like a book or a butterfly. The dish can be made by buying two smaller pieces, arranging them so that they overlap about an inch along the longer side, then pounding the overlap as well as the steaks themselves. Even supermarkets will do the butterflying and pounding when asked well ahead of time.

Shrimp with Green Sauce (page 170) makes a fine first course. Then serve the Braciola and the pasta, followed by a green salad and a light dessert like Zabaglione (page 184). A white wine like Frascati or Verdicchio will suit the shrimp, a full red like Barolo or Valpolicella will serve for the Braciola and pasta.

THE PASTA

Any kind of spaghetti, macaroni, or noodles.

2 pounds round steak or
    shoulder beef, pounded
    ¼ inch thick
¼ cup white raisins
1 garlic clove, minced
2 tablespoons pine nuts
salt and pepper

Spread the beef out flat. If two pieces are used, overlap them on the long side by 1 inch. Pound the overlap. Soak the raisins in hot water for 10 minutes; drain and spread on the meat. Strew the garlic and pine nuts evenly over the meat, and sprinkle salt and freshly ground pepper over all. Roll up, jelly-roll fashion, and tie with string in enough places to keep it together.

141

PASTA PRONTO!

¼ cup olive oil
1 medium yellow onion,
   finely chopped

In a heavy, lidded, flameproof casserole (preferably enameled ironware) heat the oil, and brown the roll well on all sides. When it is thoroughly browned, spoon out all but a tablespoon of fat and add the onions, stirring and cooking them until they are soft, but not brown.

2 large cans (2-pounds
   3-ounces each) Italian
   tomatoes, forced through
   a sieve or food mill
1 can tomato paste
2 tomato-paste cans water
2 tablespoons sugar
2 teaspoons salt
½ teaspoon freshly ground
   black pepper
2 teaspoons dried basil

Add all the rest of the ingredients and bring to a simmer. Cook, partially covered, on very low heat for 2½ hours, or until the beef is tender. Turn the roll occasionally during cooking. Check the seasoning, skim off fat, and remove the meat to a hot platter. Remove string and serve the meat sliced into one-inch slices with some sauce spooned over it, and more sauce in a bowl for the spaghetti or noodles. Serve grated Parmesan in another bowl.

VARIATIONS

—Mix the raisins, garlic, and nuts given in the recipe with the following ingredients, to make a more substantial filling:

¼ pound sweet or hot Italian
   sausage, skinned and
   crumbled
½ cup fresh fine bread crumbs
¼ cup chopped fresh parsley
¼ cup grated Parmesan cheese
1 hard-cooked egg, mashed
¼ teaspoon salt
½ teaspoon freshly ground black
   pepper

Spread the mixture on the beef, roll and tie, and proceed with the recipe as given. For this version, a slightly larger piece of meat could be used—2½ to 3 pounds—which, of course, would serve more people—6 to 8.

142

Scallopine Marsala
Veal Marsala

for 4

5 MINUTES

Veal Marsala is the best thing in the world to serve with pasta. Or so it seems, when you are having some. The scallops of veal suit any kind of spaghetti and any sauce, and should be served on the plate with the spaghetti. If the sauce has no tomatoes in it, white wines like Frascati or California Chenin Blanc taste best; if it does, red wine's the thing—a Chianti or a Nebbiolo or a California Gamay. A green salad with oil and vinegar goes well with it, followed by fresh fruit for dessert. In Italian neighborhoods, one can occasionally find *rugula*, or rocket, for the salad: the green is hard to clean but worth the effort.

This is a simple recipe for veal with Marsala. There are more elegant versions, but none better. The one below tastes best with pastas that are served with sauces that do not contain tomatoes.

Veal scallops are best when cut from the leg, although the loin meat and meat from the rib is often used. The butcher will pound the little pieces of veal, but rarely enough. The simplest way is to place them between two sheets of wax paper, and pound them flat with a cleaver or the bottom of a bottle, being careful not to hit them so hard that holes are made in the scallops. When well flattened they should be less than a quarter-inch thick. The scallops cans be sprinkled lightly with flour, which is smoothed in with the hand; this helps them brown, but the step is not essential. They should be dried thoroughly, and sprinkled with salt and pepper. No more than four should be cooked at once, as true scallops cook as quickly as pancakes. With pasta as the accompaniment, one or two scallops per person is a sufficient serving.

THE PASTA
Any kind at all.

4–8 veal scallops, flattened	Dry scallops on paper towel.
½ teaspoon salt	
¼ teaspoon freshly ground pepper	Sprinkle flattened scallops with seasonings, rubbing them into the surface.
4 tablespoons butter	Heat the butter and oil in a large skillet
2 tablespoons olive oil	over a fairly high flame. When the foam has almost completely subsided, add the scallops and cook for 2 minutes on each side. They may be turned once in a

while, and are not apt to brown much. Place on a warm platter.

¼ cup finely chopped
    shallots, scallions,
    or onions

¼ cup Marsala

¼ cup chopped fresh parsley
½ lemon

Add the shallots or onions to the pan, and when they have just begun to turn golden, pour in the Marsala. Turn the heat high and stir briskly to loosen any bits stuck to the pan. When the wine has reduced by half, and there seems to be only a scant teaspoon left for each scallop, pour the pan gravy over the scallops. Sprinkle with chopped parsley, squeeze a few drops of lemon on each, and serve.

VARIATIONS

—The same method can be used for cooking thin slices of flattened round steak. Sliced mushrooms may be added with the onion.

—Chicken livers, shrimp, and sea scallops can be prepared this way, and will cook in less than 3 minutes; they should be stirred constantly.

—Boned, flattened chicken breasts are delicious when prepared like Veal Marsala. In a skillet, over moderate heat, melt 4 tablespoons of butter and one of olive oil. Sprinkle 4 boned chicken breasts with salt and pepper. When the butter foams, dump in 2 tablespoons chopped shallots, scallions, or onions and ¼ pound chopped mushrooms. Place the chicken breasts in the skillet and cook 3–5 minutes, turning them over occasionally. The breasts are done when they spring back when touched. Remove the breasts to a warm plate. Pour into the skillet ¼ cup Marsala, white wine, or dry or sweet vermouth. Turn up the heat, squeeze half a lemon over the bubbling mixture, and when the liquid has partially boiled away, pour it over the breasts. Serve at once.

Breaded Pork Chops
for 4–6   10–15 MINUTES

Pork chops always seem just right with pasta, particularly those with simple herb or tomato sauces. Unfortunately, American pork has changed in recent years. It is produced without much fat, so that thin chops are dry and hard when grilled or sautéed, and thick ones that require long cooking are stringy and taste-less. If you can ignore the dryness and the stringiness, pork chops still taste good with pasta.

The chops can be seasoned as they cook, with salt and pepper and other herbs—oregano, sage, rosemary, savory. Savory and rosemary season best when fine, and need to be ground with the back of a spoon or in a mortar. A touch of garlic can be obtained by rubbing the chops with a clove before cooking, or by cook-ing the garlic clove with the chops until it begins to brown, then removing it.

The chops are served with the pasta. A green vegetable might also be served, particularly string beans, artichoke hearts, or zuc-chini. Olives and Oranges (page 176) might be served as an ap-petizer with cocktails; consider lemon sherbet for dessert. A light red wine like Bardolino or Valpolicella or California Pinot Noir is a good accompaniment to the meal.

THE PASTA
Thin spaghetti or noodles.

½ teaspoon salt

1 piece of garlic, the size
   of a pea

½ cup fine dry bread
   crumbs

1 tablespoon finely chopped
   fresh parsley

¼ cup grated Parmesan
   cheese

¼ teaspoon pepper

½ teaspoon oregano

6 thin pork chops, about
   ½ inch thick

1 egg, beaten

2 tablespoons olive oil

1 tablespoon butter

Mash the garlic with the salt, and mix with the crumbs, parsley, cheese, pepper, and oregano.

Wipe the chops with damp paper towel, and dip each one in the beaten egg, then in the crumb mixture. If possible, refrigerate for half an hour, or more.

In a skillet, heat the oil and butter, and when the foam has subsided, put in the chops. Turn when the first side has browned lightly. Brown the other side lightly, and continue to turn and cook until both sides are well browned.

Omelettes Aux Fines Herbes
Herb Omelets

for 4   20 MINUTES

Parmesan

Omelets are about the cheapest thing on a restaurant menu. Newcomers starting out in New York eat a lot of them, which may be why they forget about omelets later. Lucky people hit Italian restaurants early, and never forget.

There are omelets with a dollop of tomato sauce inside, or with sausages, or with that scramble of onions and peppers sautéed in oil that usually go into a hero sandwich. There are omelets with green peppers alone, and with chicken livers and bacon and onions. There are omelets with cheese—provolone or ricotta

148

or mozzarella and green onions—and more cheese sprinkled over, usually Parmesan. Many's the bachelor that courted a girl by borrowing the Italian tricks and whipping up an omelet for a little supper—with spaghetti on the side, salad and red wine.

Best of all, perhaps, is the herb omelet, with parsley and marjoram and thyme—or maybe a little oregano. Serve the pasta alongside in a butter and garlic sauce in which a little basil has steeped, fresh basil in warm weather, dried in winter—with Frascati or Soave, some antipasto at the beginning and Zabaglione (page 184) for dessert.

This isn't an Italian omelet at all, of course, but a Frenchified version using Italian ingredients—herbs, sauces, and garnishes. A particularly Italian touch is to sprinkle both omelet and pasta with cheese; sometimes the omelet receives a spoonful of tomato sauce, as well.

A real Italian *frittata* is quite different and quite filling; zucchini, eggplant, artichoke hearts, tomatoes, green or red, even potatoes, are sautéed in olive oil, then beaten eggs are poured over them and allowed to set. Sometimes the flat omelet is slipped out on a plate, then turned over into the pan. The French way is more familiar, and often preferred.

A Fines Herbes Omelet can be made with parsley alone, but the addition of freshly chopped or dried chervil, a pinch of tarragon, and chives is customary. The herbs are added to the beaten eggs when they are partly set, or are poured into the butter in the pan just before the eggs go in; more herbs can be sprinkled over the finished omelet.

An omelet pan is less than 8 inches across, with rounded, sloping sides. It is never used for cooking anything else. *Since omelets are made individually, we have presented the ingredients for a single omelet only; for four omelets, you'll need to quadruple the ingredients on hand.*

When serving omelets with pasta, the trick is to get everything on the table at once, so it helps to have someone draining and tossing and serving the pasta while you are making the omelets. If you are working alone, prepare your first omelet mixture. Then before you cook it, cook and drain the pasta. Pour the pasta into a hot bowl with the sauce recipe given below, then put in a warm oven set at about 200° to wait the few minutes it takes to make the omelets. This sounds more hectic than it is. Men don't seem to mind the bustle of cooking omelets, which gives them a sense of mastery of the intricate, but many women hate the last-minute flurry.

THE PASTA
One pound of any thin spaghetti.

THE OMELET

3 eggs
1 tablespoon water
¼ teaspoon salt
freshly ground pepper

Beat the eggs lightly with the water, only until whites and yolks are well-blended. Add the salt and a few grinds of pepper, beating a little so that the seasonings are well mixed.

2 tablespoons fresh parsley, chopped
1 teaspoon fresh chervil, chopped, or ½ teaspoon dried
½ teaspoon fresh tarragon, chopped, or pinch of dried
1 teaspoon fresh chives, chopped

Chop the herbs together. Double the amount of parsley if some of the herbs are dried or if all of them are not used. Reserve some of the herbs for sprinkling over the finished omelet.

2 tablespoons butter
¼ cup grated Parmesan cheese
or
2 tablespoons tomato sauce, warmed

Melt the butter in the omelet pan over fairly high heat, and when the foam begins to subside, pour in the herbs, turn down the heat slightly, and pour in the eggs. (You may, if you wish, stir in the herbs after you have poured in the eggs, or sprinkle herbs over the eggs as the omelet begins to set.)

150

With the back of a fork, pull the setting eggs away from the sides of the pan, so that the liquid portion can run under the eggs that are partially set. While there is still some unset mixture in the center of the pan, fold that third of the omelet nearest you over the center. Roll the folded section toward the far side of the pan and turn out on a hot plate.

If the handle of the pan is grasped palm up and tilted up as the omelet is being folded over, the omelet will roll toward the far side of the pan. If it slides and does not roll, the omelet may sprawl all over the plate when it is turned out. The best way to reshape it on the plate is with the fingers, quickly. The folding and turning can be done almost in a single gesture.

Spread a little butter on the omelet to make it glisten, sprinkle the remaining herbs over, and serve.

Some tomato sauce can be poured over the omelet, or a sprinkling of cheese, or both.

In a small saucepan over a low flame or candlewarmer, melt the stick of butter and add the oil and garlic. Sprinkle in the basil, letting it steep for at least 5 minutes. Before serving, discard the garlic.

SAUCE FOR THE PASTA

¼ pound butter

4 tablespoons olive oil

4 garlic cloves, split

1 tablespoon fresh chopped basil, or 1 teaspoon dried

NOTE

Any sauce can be used but the one above is particularly good on the pasta when it is served with herb omelets, and omelets made with cheese, mushrooms, or other vegetables.

151

Parsley-Stuffed Chickens

for 6   45–60 MINUTES

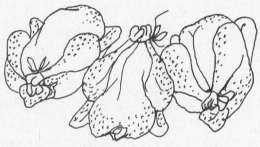

Trussed Chickens

This is a marvelously simple chicken dish that is a relative of the French way of roasting a chicken stuffed with tarragon. This one calls for parsley and some garlic. It is the nicest thing that ever happened to supermarket chicken.

Try a first course of Fettuccine al Burro or a Marinara. Some simply cooked green vegetable, dressed with butter, goes well with the main course. After a simple salad and some cheese, Biscuit Tortoni (page 183) would be a fine dessert, followed by brandy and espresso.

The chicken calls for wine. A young red wine would do—a Bardolino or Nebbiolo—but a fine old bottle would do better, a six-year-old Chianti Classico or Barolo, or a California Cabernet Sauvignon.

THE PASTA
Any kind at all.

3 whole frying chickens, about
   2½ pounds each
1 lemon, quartered
1 very large bunch parsley, or
   enough to fill chicken cav-
   ities completely
3 garlic cloves, peeled and
   halved
¾ pound butter, melted
powdered ginger
salt and pepper

Wipe the inside and outside of the chickens with damp paper towel. Rub the insides with one of the lemon wedges. Discard the lemon wedge. Wash the parsley and stuff each chicken with as much of it as the cavity will hold. Put a lemon wedge in each, under the parsley, and put 2 garlic clove halves in each, under the breasts.

Pull the skin over each opening, and tie the legs and tail pieces together to hold it closed. Turn breast side down, and with a pastry brush, paint with melted butter, covering well. When the butter has hardened, set the chickens on a rack in a shallow roasting pan, breast sides up. Paint with butter, surfaces and crevices, so the chickens are completely encased in butter. Sprinkle with ginger, salt, and pepper. Place in preheated, 475° oven for 15 minutes. Turn heat down to 375°, and cook 30–45 minutes longer, or until the chickens are tender, puffed, and golden brown.

NOTE

Chickens can be prepared ahead and refrigerated for as long as 8 hours.

CHINESE NOODLES AND OTHER FOREIGN AFFAIRS

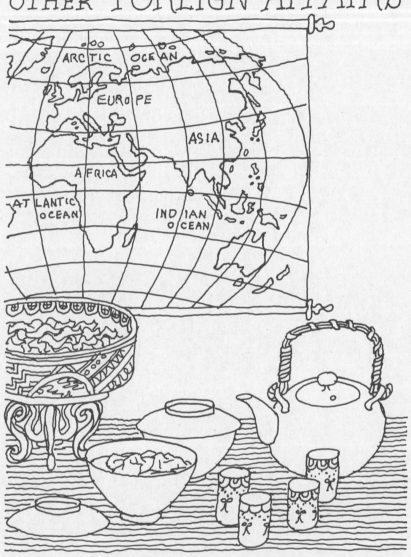

Chinese Noodles and
Other Foreign Affairs

When Marco Polo returned to Venice from the Orient in 1295, he certainly brought noodles and ways to cook them. However, in her excellent book *The Best of Italian Cooking,*[*] Nika Standen Hazelton notes an account of one Hermit William who was served macaroni around 1200. In his book *Pasta,*[†] Jack Denton Scott says records of the dough go back to 5000 B.C., and notes that the spaghetti museum in Pontedassio, near the Riviera, claims Romans ate ravioli in 1284. Furthermore, today's Romans say that those of Caesar's day had a version of macaroni, probably a kind of broad noodle like lasagne, and that the word goes back to the Greeks. Probably so, because one of the most famous (and variable) of Greek dishes is pastichio—layers of broad noodles, meat sauce, cream sauce, and sprinkles of cheese, the top layer always being the cream sauce. There's nothing like it in the Orient.

In any event, Italians certainly put holes in pasta and called it macaroni, a word that came to signify a dandy when it was introduced into London clubs

* Published by World, 1966, and in paperback by Signet, 1969.

† Published by Morrow, 1968, and in paperback by Bantam, 1970.

shortly before the American Revolution. Thin strands of pasta took over south of Rome, where spaghetti became the staple. Wide strands dominated the northern provinces, and these were the noodles that crept into northern Europe. Pasta in some form has been found in many early cultures.

A wall of dumplings stretches across Europe, and noodles had to flank it, coming up through Vienna. It's hard to imagine a goulash without its buttered noodles. Often as not, a spoonful of poppy seeds is sprinkled on after the butter, and this is one of the best and simplest of pasta dishes.

There is hardly need for a recipe, but a fancy Viennese pasta dish calls for lightly browning half a cup of slivered almonds in a couple of tablespoons of butter and adding two tablespoons of poppy seeds; toss with half a pound of boiled noodles. It's a marvelous accompaniment for all sorts of stews and pot roasts and sensational with chicken. The Hungarians sometimes add a teaspoonful of paprika, or use chopped walnuts and leave out the poppy seeds.

Noodles worked east and west from Vienna, and climbed the Alps as well, often cooked in stock to replace dumplings, and appearing in a variety of casseroles. The Germans were partial to buttered noodles with caraway seeds, but often enough they just added varying amounts of cream, butter, and cheese, plus a generous sprinkling of nutmeg, with the salt and pepper. Plain boiled noodles were often tossed with sour cream to become a side dish. In the Balkans and further west, cupfuls of sour cream and cottage cheese were combined with the noodles, often topped with crumbled bacon or bits of ham.

With the growth of restaurants in the nineteenth century, noodles and spaghetti and macaroni entered the international cuisine.

The French used pasta in various combinations with their range of sauces, even taking to stuffing fowl with noodle dressing. The Poles sprinkled buttered noodles with bread crumbs browned in butter. The Swiss put noodles in a baking dish covered with warmed cream and a grating of Parmesan, then browned the dish in the oven.

Some dishes got quite fancy. *Spaghetti à l'impériale* involved a dice of foie gras, truffles, and buttered mushrooms, bound with a sauce based on stock and laced with Madeira. *Spaghetti à la piémontaise* called for thinly sliced white truffles, plenty of butter and Parmesan, and tomato sauce served on the side. *Spaghetti à la Vénetienne* was the same, and a sauce based on stock added in place of the tomato sauce, plus a julienne of mushrooms, chicken, and ham. And *spaghetti à la milanaise,* replaced the chicken with tongue and used tomato purée for the sauce.

Anything that went into a pastry shell also was poured onto spaghetti or noodles, preparing the way for that inevitable version of chicken à la king called Tetrazzini. Named after a coloratura famous in the first decade of this century, it's a bland dish that's hard to get much taste into, and is therefore good for multitudes. It is easy to serve hot, chefs are forever adding bits of this and that from the repertoire above to perk it up; and some people dote on it. Family cooks like it because it can be made on the stove, in a chafing dish, or browned in the oven—and because it uses up leftovers.

Chicken Tetrazzini

for 4–6   15 MINUTES

Dishes were named for royalty and celebrities around the turn of the twentieth century; opera singers were frequently so honored because they enjoyed eating so much. The dishes could be elaborate concoctions or as simple as Melba toast.

This recipe was invented probably in Chicago for the great coloratura soprano Luisa Tetrazzini, and of course was one of the opera star's favorite dishes. Chicken Tetrazzini is a creamy combination of chicken and pasta, turned into a casserole. Here it is presented as a sauce for spaghetti, made while the spaghetti is cooking, stirred in, and served at once. In the variations following the recipe, it is given in its casserole form.

A good first course before Chicken Tetrazzini is melon with prosciutto. A crisp salad of endive and watercress would go well after, with Biscuit Tortoni (page 183) for dessert. A light red wine like Bardolino or Nebbiolo, a white Soave, or a California Chenin Blanc could be served with the main course.

THE PASTA

Any thin spaghetti.

158

3 tablespoons butter

¼ pound mushrooms, sliced

3 tablespoons flour

2 cups chicken stock or
canned chicken broth

¼ teaspoon white pepper

pinch of nutmeg

2 cups cooked chicken or
turkey, in 1-inch pieces

1 small green pepper, seeded
and chopped

4 pimientos, chopped

½ cup heavy cream

2 tablespoons Amontillado or
cream sherry

salt to taste

1 POUND SPAGHETTI

SET 6 QUARTS WATER TO BOIL, WITH 2 TABLESPOONS SALT; THIS MAY TAKE HALF AN HOUR.

In a heavy saucepan, heat the butter. When it stops foaming, put in the mushrooms, stirring to coat with butter. Remove from the heat and sprinkle in the flour, stirring carefully until it no longer shows white. Add a little of the chicken stock or broth and stir until smooth. Return to heat and add the rest of the stock gradually. Add the pepper and nutmeg, and, stirring constantly, simmer for 5 minutes, or until sauce thickens.

PUT SPAGHETTI IN THE BOILING WATER AND COOK 8–9 MINUTES, OR UNTIL DONE, BUT STILL QUITE FIRM.

Add chicken or turkey, green pepper, and pimientos to the sauce and cook 5 minutes. Add cream and sherry. Heat but do not boil. Check seasoning, adding salt to taste.

1 cup freshly grated Parmesan,
Gruyère, fontina,
or Sardo cheese

Drain spaghetti and turn into a warm bowl. Add some of the cheese and all of the sauce, toss gently. Serve the rest of the cheese on the side.

VARIATIONS

—To make the dish in its casserole form, cook only ½ pound of spaghetti. Put the cooked spaghetti into a buttered casserole, or

159

divide among individual ones. Add half the cheese to the sauce, and pour over the spaghetti. Sprinkle with the rest of the cheese and place, uncovered, in preheated, 350° oven for 20 minutes, or until lightly browned. Serves 4.

—For another casserole version, place cooked broccoli in the bottom of a buttered casserole. Put the chicken or turkey, in slices, over the broccoli. Add half the cheese to the sauce, and pour over. Sprinkle with the rest of the cheese, and bake as above. Serve the spaghetti on the side, buttered. In this case noodles would be even better than spaghetti.

Noodle cookery has an enormous range in Europe and Asia. Dumpling country takes squares or rounds of the noodle dough, places a spoonful of something tasty on them and folds the dough over and then boils them in salted water, so that ravioli becomes *kerplach* in Jewish cookery and *pelmeny* in Russian—cousins of the endless number of baked turnovers that are known all over Europe. All boiled turnovers surely hark back to the *wonton* of Chinese cookery.

The Japanese call noodles *udon* when they are large and *soba* when they are thin, like tagliatelle or fettuccine. Some are made from buckwheat, which is gray; others contain spinach, and are a familiar green. Japan's vendors sell *soba* from carts, covered with broth and seasoned with *shōyu,* the liquid salt-and-pepper of Japan that is soy sauce. Scallions are sprinkled over the top. Larger *udon* is sautéed in vegetable oil with *shōyu,* and the scallions are stirred in at the last minute. All sorts of things diced or shredded or cut in thin strips for a julienne, are stirred in or sprinkled over—cooked pork or chicken, string beans, bean sprouts, mushrooms, peas, cucumbers, carrots. A minced garlic clove may be added, or a couple of tablespoons of sherry, a grating of ginger, or some of the juice from preserved ginger, chutney, or a red pepper powder called *togarishi*. Cooked in stock or sautéed in oil, variations are endless. Sometimes the noodles are served cold; the cold cooking liquid is used as a sauce, in which one dips a chopstick full of cold noodles. Noodles can be, and are, substituted for rice in any number of Oriental dishes.

Perhaps the simplest service of all is to heat a cup of stock and a tablespoon of *shōyu* in a chafing dish with some mushrooms and scallions. When the mixture is hot, these are poured over bowls of hot noodles that have been cooked in stock.

All this stems, of course, from Chinese cookery, and to give a better idea, we include here a recipe adapted from Jim Lee's *Chinese Cook Book*.* One of his recipes leads inevitably to another, opening an enormous realm.

One can get to believe that pasta is a way of life. In China and Japan—and Italy—it is.

*Published by Harper and Row in 1969.

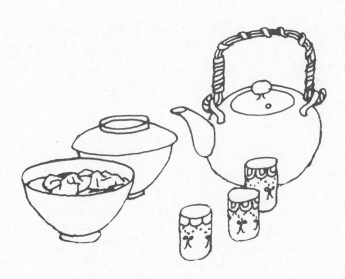

Shrimp Lo Mein

for 4 20 MINUTES

The Chinese use cooked noodles to make many dishes. *Chow Mein* is cooked noodles fried in vegetable oil, a nest of them being browned in less than an inch of oil and then turned over. *Voy Mein* is cooked noodles simmered in stock and then drained. *Yee Foo Mein* is cooked noodles that have been fried,

162

then simmered in boiling salted water, and drained. *Lo Mein* is cooked noodles stir-fried with various ingredients. Other methods call for piling the added ingredients on top. Each way tastes unique, and there are Chinese restaurants that specialize in nothing but noodle dishes.

The dish presented here calls for cooked shrimp but is much better when made with dried shrimp that have to be soaked in water for an hour, like dried Chinese mushrooms, both of which are available only in Chinese shops. Cooked chicken, veal, or beef—all cut in julienne strips an eighth of an inch thick, a quarter of an inch wide and two inches long—can be used. Bean sprouts and soy sauce can be found in most supermarkets. Fresh ginger may have to be sought for, but ginger preserved in syrup or in chutney is easy to find.

Shrimp Lo Mein can be made on the top of the stove, in a wok, a chafing dish, or an electric skillet; the skillet is the easiest. Try two or three variations with different meat, fish, or seafood, to see how you like them.

Tea, or glasses of chilled dry Fino or Amontillado sherry or a white wine like Soave or California Chenin Blanc can be served. This could be followed by lemon sherbet, or even kumquats or melon, and almond cookies.

THE PASTA
Thin egg noodles, about a 12-ounce package. These should be cooked first and kept warm, with a little oil added to keep from sticking together.

¾ cup oil
⅛ teaspoon salt
1 slice fresh or preserved ginger, about one inch in diameter, chopped (this is about 1 tablespoon)

Heat a heavy, lidded skillet hot and dry. Put in 3 tablespoons of the oil and the salt. Add the ginger and garlic, and as soon as they are golden, add all the vegetables. Cook, stirring, for 1 minute. Add the sherry, cover and cook for another

163

PASTA PRONTO!

1 garlic clove, minced

2 cups French-cut green beans, cooked

2 cups bean sprouts, drained

3 scallions, cut into 2-inch slivers

4 medium Chinese mushrooms, soaked and shredded; or ¼ pound fresh mushrooms, sliced; or 1 can sliced mushrooms, drained

2 tablespoons Fino sherry

4 cups noodles, cooked

2 cups shrimp, cooked

¼ cup soy sauce

1 teaspoon sugar

minute. Remove from the heat; drain and reserve vegetables.

Clean the skillet and heat dry again. Put in the rest of the oil, and turn the heat to medium. Add the noodles and stir constantly for 2–3 minutes to coat the noodles thoroughly and to heat them through. Add the shrimp and the reserved vegetables. Mix well. Add the soy sauce and sugar, stirring to coat everything evenly. Serve on a warm platter, garnished with parsley sprigs.

ANTIPASTI, INSALATI
AND DESSERTS

Antipasti, Insalati, and Desserts

I talians are blessed with a constant bounty of fresh vegetables. Furthermore, they have raised to the level of art the pickling and spicing of fresh foods so that greens taste almost better in the preserved state. Italians are also artisans of smoking, salting, and canning. Unique sausages are found in every part of the country, Bologna and salami being the most famous. All this native skill comes together in the platter of antipasti that starts off many Italian meals.

Antipasti vary to suit the pasta and other courses to follow. The salad course, or insalati, generally should contrast what is served as antipasti. We present a selection of antipasti and insalati to be served as complements to the other recipes in the book.

167

Antipasto

Perhaps the best known first course to precede pasta is the handsome platter of good things to eat called simply antipasto (before the pasta). With its wide variety of tastes, textures, and colors, antipasto is the perfect introduction, properly whetting the appetite.

Many of the items for antipasto can be bought in cans or jars and kept in stock on your kitchen shelf:

sardines	artichoke hearts, marinated
anchovies	olives, green and black
tuna fish	hot chili pickles
pimientos	marinated mushrooms
capers	pickled beets

Vegetables on an antipasto plate should be sprinkled with oil, vinegar, salt, and pepper. If a vegetable is cooked first, it should still be firm when served. Some vegetables used often in antipasto are:

> carrots in thin strips, raw or cooked
> sliced cooked potatoes with a sprinkling of chopped scallions
> raw or cooked small broccoli and cauliflower buds
> whole green beans, cooked
> red and green peppers, in strips
> scallions
> tomatoes in wedges
> radishes
> celery
> fennel in thin lengthwise strips
> watercress

Meats can be:

> sliced Genoa salami or pepperoni sausage
> prosciutto or other good ham in thin slices, rolled up

With hard-cooked eggs, in wedges or sliced, some Italian cheese like provolone, and a little lettuce, you have a marvelous selection from which to form an attractive antipasto. Offer olive oil and good wine vinegar and the pepper mill, for people to dress their own individual plates of antipasto.

Green Sauce

This bright green sauce is a fresh cool dip for raw vegetables, shrimp, and breadsticks, and it is particularly good before pasta. It is hard to measure things like unchopped fresh basil and parsley, but it doesn't matter. The sauce is essentially a French dressing plus handfuls of fresh greens and a few scallions. Whether made in the blender or even by hand, it is surprising how much green bulk can be incorporated into the oil and vinegar.

⅓ cup olive oil, salad oil,
    or a combination of both
2 tablespoons wine or cider
    vinegar
¼ teaspoon salt
a few grinds of the pepper
    mill
¼ teaspoon dry mustard, or
    1 teaspoon Dijon mustard
1 cup fresh basil leaves,
    loosely packed
1 cup fresh parsley, without
    stems, loosely packed
4–6 scallions with green tops,
    chopped

Put all ingredients into a blender and blend until smooth and bright green. To do by hand, chop basil, parsley, and onions very finely, and mix thoroughly with the rest of the ingredients. Makes about ¾ cup of sauce.

NOTE

If fresh basil is unavailable, use 1 tablespoon dried basil with a cup of fresh watercress, or another cup of fresh parsley.

Bagna Cauda
Hot Bath

This extremely flavorful "Hot Bath," or hot dip, for crisp vegetables and breadsticks is the Anchovy Sauce for spaghetti (page 65), with slight differences in the proportions and without the olives and parsley.

Any raw crisp vegetables can be used for dips, but the easiest to handle with the fingers are ones that can be cut in long thin strips, such as celery, endive, Chinese cabbage, romaine, fennel, cucumber, scallions. For spearing on a fork, try radishes, cauliflower and broccoli buds, cooked artichoke hearts, raw mushrooms, and cherry tomatoes.

½ cup butter
¼ cup olive oil
4 garlic cloves, slivered
1 2-ounce can anchovy fillets,
  chopped

In a small saucepan, heat together the butter and oil and garlic. Allow the mixture to simmer for 15 minutes without quite boiling. Add the anchovies and stir until they dissolve. Serve in the saucepan, kept warm over a candle warmer, with the bread sticks and vegetables for dipping. Vegetables can be crisped by standing them in iced water for an hour. Makes about ¾ cup of sauce.

171

La Caponata

for 6–8   20–25 MINUTES

A magical mush of vegetables with a slightly sweet-sour taste, La Caponata, is served cold. It can be used as a first course alone or as part of the antipasto, with bread; instead of salad or vegetables, with simply cooked or broiled meats; or for a buffet, as a sort of relish. The Sicilian dish is based on eggplant and zucchini, like its French cousin, *ratatouille*. Other ingredients are varied freely. The garlic can be increased or left out, the seasoning can be salt and pepper alone. A medium chopped green pepper and half a pound of sliced mushrooms might be added or substituted for the zucchini; these would go in at the same time as the onions. The dish goes well with bland pastas, but it is also excellent with slices of cold roasts, chicken, or ham. It can be served with white wines like Frascati or reds that are light or rough, like Vesuvio or Bardolino or a Zinfandel from California.

1 large eggplant or 2 small
   ones, cut into 1-inch cubes
1 medium zucchini, cut into
   ½–¾ inch cubes
½ cup olive oil, more
   if needed
salt and pepper to taste

If the eggplant is young and fresh, do not peel; otherwise peel. Cut into cubes. Lightly scrape the zucchini and cube. Heat the olive oil in a skillet and quickly cook the eggplant and zucchini, a few pieces at a time, until they are lightly brown. Remove the pieces as they are done to a lidded, flameproof casserole. Sprinkle with salt and pepper.

2 medium onions
1 garlic clove, minced
1 cup diced celery
1 1-pound can Italian
   tomatoes, sieved
½ teaspoon basil
½ teaspoon oregano

In the skillet, slowly cook the onions until they are limp but not brown, using more oil if none remains in the pan. Add the garlic, celery, tomatoes (which have been forced through a strainer or food mill), and the basil and oregano. Simmer 15 minutes and add to the vegetables in the casserole.

2 tablespoons capers, drained
2 tablespoons pine nuts or
   slivered almonds
8 pitted black olives, coarsely
   chopped
8 pitted green olives, coarsely
   chopped

Add the capers, nuts, and olives.

2 tablespoons sugar
¼ cup wine vinegar
½ teaspoon salt
¼ teaspoon pepper

In a small saucepan, warm the vinegar and melt the sugar in it. Add the salt and pepper and stir the mixture into the casserole. Cover and cook over very low heat for 20 minutes, stirring occasionally. The Caponata should be thick, but if it gets too dry, add a little hot water. Cool and chill.

Scallops with Pernod

for 4–6   5 MINUTES

4 tablespoons butter
¾ pound raw bay scallops,
   or sea scallops cut in half
¼ teaspoon salt
3–4 grinds of the pepper mill
1 tablespoon Pernod or Pec
¼ cup finely chopped fresh
   parsley
lime juice

Melt the butter in a chafing dish or skillet. Dry the scallops on paper towel, and put them into the butter when the foam subsides. Stir and cook 2–3 minutes, just until they become opaque. Sprinkle with salt and pepper, stir in the Pernod or Pec and the parsley, squeeze over the juice of half a lime, and serve immediately. Use as an appetizer on small plates or shells. Breadsticks are a good accompaniment.

Green Salad

In general, a simple salad of varied greens, with some crisp raw vegetables for accents and a slightly sharp dressing, is the best to have with pasta dishes. The dressing given here, similar to a French dressing, has a little bit of garlic, a touch of paprika, some basil and the not-so-French addition of a pinch of sugar. The greens can be as varied as your market can supply, but don't forget endive and raw spinach. The crisp accents can be radishes, small cauliflower or broccoli florets, slivers of raw turnip, rings of red or Spanish onion (allowed to stand in ice water for an hour to crisp), cucumbers, celery, fennel, grated or slivered raw carrots.

Italian Dressing

for 4

piece of garlic the size
  of a pea
¼ teaspoon salt
1–2 tablespoons wine vinegar
⅛ teaspoon finely ground
  black pepper
½ teaspoon dried basil
¼ teaspoon paprika
¼ teaspoon dry mustard
pinch of sugar
6 tablespoons olive oil

Mash the garlic with the salt, and add with the rest of the seasonings to the vinegar. Start with 1 tablespoon of vinegar, add more later to taste. Beat in the oil just before using. Makes about ½ cup.

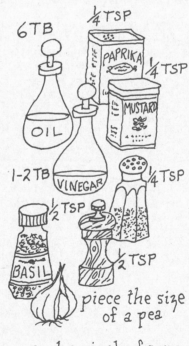

... and a pinch of sugar

Oranges and Olives

for 4

Some unexpected combinations are delicious, and this is one. Drain a pound of black olives of the brine they have been packed in, pour them into a bowl with some olive oil—about ¼ cup—and squeeze over them the juice of a lemon. Slice an orange—but don't peel it—and add to the bowl, giving everything a few stirs. Serve Oranges and Olives with drinks before dinner, or in place of the salad course. Or simply set out a plate with a bottle of red wine for a midmorning or afternoon snack; Oranges and Olives seems to have a special affinity for red wine.

Plain Bean Salad

Cooked green beans alone make an excellent salad to accompany some pasta dishes. Gently tossed with the Italian Dressing and a sprinkle of chopped fresh parsley, the beans should be allowed to stand for at least half an hour to absorb the flavor of the dressing. When the pasta dish is a simple one, or is used as a side dish with a roast, grilled fish or plain chops, the bean salad can have these extra enrichments: crumbled crisp bacon, slivered almonds, chopped green onions.

Mixed Bean Salad

for 4–6

A mixture of different kinds of canned beans makes a colorful salad, although it is rather hearty for a rich pasta dish. It has the great advantage of keeping well for a few days; in fact it improves with standing, so it is worth making in quantity. This recipe makes about 2 quarts (about 8 cups).

1 1-pound can cut green beans
1 1-pound can cut wax beans
1 1-pound can red kidney
  beans
1 1-pound can garbanzo beans
  (chick peas)
1 green pepper, finely chopped
½ cup finely chopped fresh
  parsley
1 large red onion, chopped or
  in rings, or 4–6 scallions
  with green tops, chopped

1 cup Italian Dressing
  (page 175)

Drain the green and wax beans. Drain and rinse the kidney and garbanzo beans. Mix the beans gently with the rest of the ingredients and the dressing. Allow to stand for an hour in the refrigerator, stirring carefully once or twice. Taste before serving; more salt, pepper, or vinegar might be needed, or you might want to add more dressing.

177

Tomato Salads

Tomatoes are not entirely desirable in a salad that is served with pasta containing tomatoes in its sauce. Otherwise, tomatoes supply cooling moistness and appetizing color in the usual green salad with an Italian dressing. (For the red touch in a green salad without tomatoes, use chopped pimientos.)

The best possible way to use tomatoes when they are at their most perfect—at the height of the season and when fresh basil is available—is to have them sliced, all by themselves with chopped fresh basil sprinkled over them. Don't use any dressing at all.

When the tomatoes are not quite so good, they can be sliced or cut into wedges, sprinkled with oil and vinegar, salt and pepper, and finely chopped fresh parsley.

For a pleasant change of menu, especially in summer, a salad can be the substantial part of the meal, after a first course of pasta with a very simple sauce, such as Al Burro (page 44) or Aglio e Olio (page 48). This kind of meal is perfect for luncheon or supper outdoors, the pasta turned with its sauce in a chafing dish at the table, the beautiful salad waiting to be tossed, wine bottles and glasses glinting in the sun, and golden loaves of French or Italian bread ready for slicing. Good any time of the year, these main-course salads do equally well for party or family meals, with endless possibilities for glamorous presentation and plenty of nourishment to satisfy a conscientious mother.

Two main-course salad recipes are given here, with a long list of other possibilities, so the cook can feel free to experiment as taste and the larder dictate. Mayonnaise and sour-cream dressings are omitted because they are not suitable for a salad to follow pasta.

Since the pasta recipes in this book are for 6 servings when served as a first course, the salad recipes are also for 6 servings.

Salade Niçoise

for 4–6

salad greens—equal parts of romaine, Boston or lime-
    stone, bibb, or leaf lettuce
3 medium tomatoes, sliced
1 green pepper, thinly sliced in rings
1 red onion, thinly sliced in rings
3 hard-cooked eggs, sliced
1 2-ounce can anchovy fillets, drained
10 pitted green olives
10 pitted black olives
1 6½-ounce can tuna fish, drained
2 tablespoons capers, drained
¼ cup finely chopped fresh parsley

French Dressing

2–3 tablespoons wine or cider
    vinegar
1 teaspoon Dijon mustard
¼ teaspoon salt
¼ teaspoon freshly ground
    black pepper
9 tablespoons olive oil,
    or part olive oil and
    part vegetable oil

Add the seasonings to 2 tablespoons vinegar. Beat in the oil, check seasoning, and add more vinegar and salt to taste. Arrange the ingredients in the order given, in a wide shallow salad bowl. Pour the dressing over the salad, but do not toss until serving time.

Chef's Salad

for 4–6

salad greens—equal parts of romaine, Boston or lime- stone, bibb, or leaf lettuce
2 stalks celery, finely chopped
½ pound Swiss cheese, in ½-inch dice
1 small cucumber, peeled and sliced
¼ pound cooked ham, diced, or in thin slivers, 2 inches long
6 hard-cooked eggs, sliced, in wedges, or yolks crumbled and whites chopped
6 radishes, sliced
4 scallions with green tops, chopped
1 small green pepper, chopped
¼ cup finely chopped fresh parsley

Arrange the ingredients in the order given, in a salad bowl, preferably a wide shallow one. Pour ¾ cup Italian Dressing (page 175) over the salad, but do not toss until serving time.

VARIATIONS

—Chef's Salad is infinitely variable. Any of the following ingredients can be used to vary the recipe given, or to make new combinations.

tomatoes, sliced or in wedges
raw mushrooms, sliced
watercress
avocado slices, with a sprinkle of lemon to prevent discoloration
raw carrots, slivered or grated
cooked artichokes, plain or marinated
chives
bean sprouts

raisins, plumped in hot water for 10 minutes
apples, diced
seeded grapes
nuts: pine nuts, slivered almonds, chopped walnuts

olives, green or black
pimientos
capers
pickles, sweet or sour, chopped
pickled beets

anchovy fillets, whole or chopped
shrimp, crabmeat, lobster
cooked chicken or turkey, diced
bacon, crisp and crumbled
chipped beef, shredded
cheese other than Swiss: Feta, Cheddar, Gruyère, Gouda, Edam

Italians adore desserts. Almost everybody does. Much of the time, an Italian will make a dessert of fresh fruit, perhaps with cheese. Few things taste so refreshing after a meal that include pasta.

After a few days of such simple delight, however, the mouth begins to water for something more. We have included some simple Italian desserts here that seem to go particularly well after pasta. For wild delights like rich pastry an Italian may succumb to the wonders of the pastry shops. With so many Italian bakeries spread around the country, indulgent Americans might do the same. All the desserts here are light, or small, or both.

Fruit

Fruit may be the best of all desserts. It is certainly the lightest. A bowl of fruits in season, pears and apples peeled and eaten with cheese and red wine, peaches and berries eaten with sweet white wines and champagnes is a splendid way to end a meal. The sweet white wines might be the sauternes of France, or the Spätlesen or Auslesen of the Rhine, made from selected Riesling grapes picked late, so that they are full of sugar. Italy has a gamut of dessert wines, less grand, made from dried grapes and called *passito*. There is one from every region, and sparkling wines, as well, perhaps the best being Asti Spumante.

And then there is sweet vermouth and Marsala, sweetened wines that approach 20 percent in alcohol content. These are marvelous poured over berries or sliced fruits shortly before serving, as much as a tablespoon of wine per portion. Occasionally, one wants a sharper taste, from distillates like kirsch, made from cherries, or Mirabelle, made from plums. The Italians have sweeter liqueurs, also laved on sliced fruits or berries; Maraschino, which is brightly sweet with the taste of cherries, or golden Strega or Fior d'Alpi, or anisette. Anisette tastes of licorice, and is both dry and sweet. The dry versions may be best on fruits. The only thing to do is try them all, one after another. It is a pleasant experiment.

Biscuit Tortoni

for 6–8   5 MINUTES

1 cup heavy cream
¼ cup confectioner's sugar
1 egg white, stiffly beaten
½ cup ground toasted almonds
  or almond cookie crumbs
1 tablespoon Marsala or cream
  sherry

Whip the cream until it begins to stiffen. Beat in the sugar, a little at a time, and beat until stiff. Fold in the beaten egg white, wine, and almonds or crumbs, reserving a sprinkling for the top. Fill 6–8 paper dessert cups, and sprinkle with reserved almonds or crumbs. Freeze until firm.

Zabaglione
Custard with Marsala

for 4   15 MINUTES

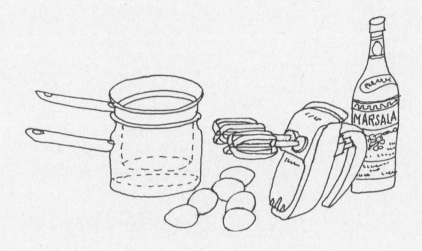

This light and lovely custard is served hot, as soon as it is made. It could be made at the table in a chafing dish if the pan is not too wide and shallow. In principle, Zabaglione is a custard made with an equal number of egg yolks, tablespoons of Marsala, and sugar. We have included one of the egg whites for extra fluffiness. If cream sherry is used instead of the Marsala it becomes a Spanish flan, equally delicious.

184

5 egg yolks plus one whole
  egg
6 tablespoons sugar
6 tablespoons Marsala

Bring a little water to simmer in the bottom of a double boiler. In the top part, away from the heat, beat the eggs and sugar until pale and almost fluffy. Now put the pan over the simmering water, but not touching it, and continue beating, adding the Marsala gradually. Beat until it is hot and thick, thick enough to hold its shape in a spoon. This may take as long as 10 minutes. Spoon into dessert dishes or parfait glasses, and serve immediately.

Poached Pears with Marsala

for 4–6   40 MINUTES

4–6 whole ripe firm pears,
   peeled, stems left on
2 cups water
1 cup sugar
4 whole cloves
1 2-inch stick of cinnamon
1 tablespoon lemon juice
4–6 tablespoons Marsala

Choose a heavy, lidded saucepan, or flameproof casserole that will hold the pears nicely in one layer. Cook the water, sugar and spices in it for 5 minutes. Add the lemon juice and pears. Cover and cook slowly until pears are tender but not mushy, at least 30 minutes, turning from time to time. Cool and chill in the liquid. To serve, remove pears from the liquid and pour a tablespoon or more of Marsala over each serving.

For a syrupy sauce, remove the pears when done, and cook the liquid over high heat until it is thick and about half cooked away. Add a tablespoon of Marsala per pear to the liquid, strain over the pears, cool, and chill. Serve with some of the sauce on each pear.

VARIATION

—Follow the recipe for Poached Pears with Marsala, using dry red wine instead of water and omitting the Marsala. Substitute a piece of lemon rind for the lemon juice. Cool and chill pears in the liquid. Serve with some of the liquid poured over each serving.

NOTE

Quartered, cored pears are easier to eat and take less time to cook, but they are not as attractive. Italians provide a knife and fork for whole pears.

Index

Grumello, 21
Inferno, 21
Lambrusco, 22
Maraschino, 26
Marsala, 25
Orvieto, 23
Ruta, 25
Santa Maddalena, 22
Sassella, 21
Soave, 23
Strega, 26
Valpantena, 21
Valpolicella, 21
Verdicchio, 23
Vernaccia, 23
White Lugana, 23

Petite Syrah, 24-25
Pinot Chardonnay, 24-25
Pinot Noir, 24-25
Riesling, 24
Sauvignon Blanc, 24-25
Sémillon, 24-25
Vino di Tavola, 23
Vino Tipo, 23
Zinfandel, 22-25

WINES (American)

Baco Noir, 24-25
Barbera, 23, 25
Barberone, 23
Cabernet Sauvignon, 24-25
Chenin Blanc, 24-25
Chianti, 23
Delaware, 24-25
Emerald Riesling, 24
Gamay Beaujolais, 24-25
Gewürztraminer, 24-25
Grey Riesling, 24
Grignolino, 23
Johannisberg Riesling, 24